The *In*surmountable Challenges of Africa!

By: Madiba EC

Copyright © 2019, Madiba EC,

All rights reserved

I dedicate this book to my fellow Africans and everyone out there who wakes up every day wondering where their next meal is going to come from.

There are sadly too many people suffering and I hope by just reading this book we can start believing that it is possible to change our fortunes and live better lives. You can leave comments or suggestions at https://www.makeafricabetter.info

This is not a book for teaching you how to be rich. It is about showing you that there are simpler things you can do in life that can make a huge difference.

Table of Contents

ACKNOWLEDGEMENTS 5

INTRODUCTION 7

CHAPTER 1 – EDUCATION 33

CHAPTER 2 – THE LIFE CHOICES 50

CHAPTER 3 – ARE BLACKS CURSED? 78

CHAPTER 4 – THE BLAME EPIDEMIC 97

CHAPTER 5 – CONFORMANCE 135

CHAPTER 6 – OF BREADWINNERS AND ENTITLEMENT 144

CHAPTER 7 – OF IDEAS, POTENTIAL AND FEAR OF FAILING 160

CHAPTER 7 – PRODUCTIVITY IS KING 183

CHAPTER 8 – SHORT TERM IS PLANNING TO FAIL 197

CHAPTER 9 – WE MUST FOCUS ON THE BASICS 219

CONCLUSIONS 230

BONUS CHAPTER 236

Acknowledgements

First, I would like to acknowledge my wife, Mrs Madiba BM, for her support. Marriage is not an easy institution. We've experienced our share of ups and downs, but we persevered. I think it is because she is the mature one in our marriage. I thank her for her strength. We have three beautiful children that we love to death. They keep us going. I love them, my wife loves them, we just love them.

A big shout out to my big family – my mother, siblings, my in-laws, nephews, cousins, nieces, aunts, uncles, and all of you lot. I love you all. Africans believe in family.

My friends from my former and current employer as well as my buddies that I worship with. Thank you all for your support.

I would also like to send my special thanks and appreciations to a gentleman called Panchu Markandu and his wife Sibetra. Panchu introduced me to a network marketing programme (by the way, I am neither encouraging nor discouraging you from joining any network marketing programme). I am not an active member at this stage but the knowledge I gained from being part of the programme was invaluable. I got to subscribe to educational and motivational books. And I started reading non-fiction books and I was never the same after reading the first book (titled Success Leaves Clues). The books changed my life forever. I got to know about people like Jim Rohn, Brian Tracy, Les Brown, and many others. I would never have known these great people had I not met Panchu. Thank you, Mr. & Mrs. Panchu.

Finally, I want to thank God for his blessings. To be able to sit down and write a book is a great blessing. For that, I thank His Grace for his support and guidance.

Introduction

Alright, before we go too far into this book, let me pose the following question:

> *"Why is it that wherever there are black people, there is usually a lot of suffering? True, it is not everywhere, but it is too common. Sometimes it seems like the odds are stacked against us."*

I believe I know the answer to this question. It is all down to mindset, which is shaped by the environment in which we grow up. Most of us are born under some really tough conditions and we grow up believing that that is normal. We accept mediocracy. It doesn't have to be that way. I will expand more on this throughout this book.

But, yes any place where blacks are in the majority, we see far too much suffering. We know about Africa of course where:

- Most people survive with under a dollar per day
- Communities are ravaged by wars
- Corruption is rampant

- Poor sanitation is a norm

- Crime is bad… and so on and so forth

Now, look at other cities outside Africa or even countries where the blacks are the majority and you will see a similar pattern. This is even the case in developed countries too where there is a high concentration of blacks in a city like in Chicago, for instance.

Consider the Aboriginal communities in Australia, especially in the Northern Territory. Their situation is tough. It is hard for most of these black communities. They are poor. There are high levels of crime in these areas. They are also the main beneficiaries of the welfare system. One former Australian prime minister, Mr. Tony Abbott summed up the situation for the aboriginal people when he said the following in an interview with The Weekend Australian:

> "Quite frankly there are, even today, parts of remote Australia that are like Somalia without guns."

Tony Abbott was explaining the plight of the blacks in Australia after visiting one of the aboriginal communities. The year? It was only 2013. Their situation is such that if you were to be blindfolded and flown from a poor country in

Africa and dropped there, you would think you were in another African country. Their advantage compared to blacks in Africa is that they live in a developed country where the government can afford to have them on welfare.

The situation with the African-Americans in the United States is no different. A lot of them are doing very well, no question about that. But we know about the situation in Chicago. The level of violent crime in Chicago is probably the worst in USA.

Exit America and enter Haiti or visit our brothers and sisters in Jamaica or New Papua Guinea. And guess what? The narrative is the same. The same old problems.

The question is why? Do we have a 'stunted' brain development and poor genetic composition, leading to all these issues amongst blacks especially in Africa? Is the size of our cerebrum, the part of the brain that does the thinking, smaller? I don't think there is any scientific proof around this question. But a quick search on Google returns a wide range of non-scientific answers.

I believe this is a genuine question and must be asked by blacks or Africans because it is a sensitive, politically charged question to ask and it is only fair for us the black race to challenge and prove this theory wrong. I personally don't think there is anything wrong with our genetic design nor our cerebrum. I could be biased because I am black. But I have seen millions of blacks doing very well in life.

This is a very important topic that needs some serious debating. There is no doubt about it given the situation we find ourselves in, but I will leave it at that for now because it is beyond the scope of this book. This question is easily a book topic on its own. Let me reiterate that I am a black African, hence the reason I said I could be biased in answering this question and I don't think I can be accused of being racist. I have a free pass to tell it as it is.

* * *

Consider the following stats:

- 7.7 billion – world population in 2018

- US$317 trillion – Global wealth in 2018

If this "money" was evenly distributed amongst all of humanity, young and old, each one of us would pocket about US$41,168. If this were to happen, hypothetically, where do you think we, Africans, would be 100 years later? Do you think we would be on par with the rest of the world? Maybe yes considering the amount of money in question. This would translate to about $45.3 trillion for Africa based on a population of 1.1 billion.

Let me be the bearer of the bad news. You may call me a pessimist or what you will, but I have a sneaky suspicion that the majority of our people would likely be back to where we are today; poor. I am sorry but that is how I envisage the situation. A lot of this cash would still be in Africa, but in the hands of the few greedy ones and the smart ones.

My belief is that all the money would be gone. There would be traces of it with some "white elephant" structures that were built out of excitement but serving no purpose at the moment. I am sorry for being so negative. It is happening even today where people squander their fortunes on material possessions. So, this is not a farfetched assumption. Jim Rohn once said:

> "If you took all the money in the world, divided it equally amongst all of us, it would soon be back in the old pockets!"

It is as if success and blacks repel each other while on the other hand the successful people and money are like the south and north poles of a magnet – they attract each other.

If the preceding argument is correct, that Africans would be back to where they "belong" and as poor as before, and that money usually returns to the old pockets, wouldn't you agree that money is not going to fix our problems? Of course, money helps. It is harder without money, but at the same time it doesn't mean that throwing money at a problem without a plan is a solution.

The point I am trying to make is that pumping money into our problems, African problems, without a clear strategy for the future is like pouring water into a leaking tank that discharges the same amount as what is poured in. That is exactly what is happening today in most African countries. Money is pumped into poor communities as welfare and the so-called poverty alleviation initiatives. What can we show for it? Nothing to be frank. If anything, this is just making the poor poorer and more reliant on governments. There is no accountability on how that money is spent and that leads to corruption.

I think it shows a lack of understanding when you hear people arguing that there is not enough money in Africa. We have plenty of money in Africa. There is a lot being pumped in as foreign aid as well as plenty from the African economies too (like from mining and other natural resources like oil and gas). The problem is the mismanagement of our money. We are not able to come up with strategies and initiatives that would lead to Africa or African countries being independent.

Let's look at Botswana for instance; and I will reference Botswana a bit because that's where I am from, but the principles are similar for other African nations anyway. Over the last 52 years of independence (we got independence from Britain in 1966), we have seen some incredible growth in terms of revenue from the diamonds sales and other mining proceeds. It's been over 50 years, but we still have no clue as to where the government would get money from when diamonds run out. We have no plans to diversify our economy even though we made so much money over the years. Our population is so small, but we are still failing to get the basics on how to spend the money wisely on human resources to prepare ourselves for the future. And if you read the State of the nation addresses by our presidents over the past 50 years or so, it is riddled with the same promises year after year but no action nor accountability. The economy has grown of course in terms of basic and expected developments like roads, hospitals, schools and those types of things. But, there is absolutely nothing to show in terms long-term sustainability and getting people trained for what is required to move the economy forward away from mining.

On the other hand, see what the Australians are doing with their proceeds from their most abundant natural resource – iron ore. Completely different – it is as different as black and white (no pun intended by the way)!

Zambia is in the same category. There was so much money out of the copper mines – you may have heard about the Copperbelt – but there is nothing to show for it. I came across the following statement about Zambia in an article written by Michael Hobbes, a Seattle-based human rights consultant and freelance journalist who was in Zambia doing some research about developing countries (or the third world countries as we are always referred). He said,

> *Zambia is not failed. It is simply very, very poor. Sixty-four percent of the population lives on less than $1 per day, 14 percent have HIV, 40 percent don't have access to clean drinking water.*

For me this sounds like a failed state. If this is not a failed state, then our situation is even worse than I thought. As far as I am concerned, a country doesn't have to go through what Somalia is going through – wars, Islamic extremists, corruption, etc – to qualify as a failed state. Failure for me is the inability to utilise the resources at your disposal to improve the living standards of your people as a government. It is just the planning, or lack of, that is putting us in this situation. So, yes, Zambia is a failed state in my eyes, and so is Zimbabwe, Democratic Republic of Congo, Swaziland, and many other African states. The theme is the same across the vast African continent.

It is for this reason that I am being *pessimistic* when it comes to my continent. Therefore, my argument that if we each had $41,000 we would have it all squandered within a generation is not farfetched given our recent history and current actions. I think we are giving some people, the so-called alt-right or the white supremacists, enough ammunition to spread their propaganda. I am not saying they have the right to be racist towards blacks. There is no excuse whatsoever for their racist propaganda. I am just telling you that our actions give them something to use against us.

We must change course and stop this craziness because Africans are better than this.

As I said before, money does help, but what matters the most is our attitude towards money. Have you ever seen African people with money? We become restless and instinctively want to spend it on flashy cars, expensive clothes, bling-bling as with the African-American. I apologise for painting everyone with the same brush because there a lot of Africans who are doing very well and behaving nothing like this, but this is true for the majority. I don't know what the cause of this craziness is. Maybe it is because we have suffered for so long that given an opportunity (of having cash) the first instinct is to spend it; enjoy the moment because we don't believe it would last.

We are reckless spenders even at government level and the Chinese for instance, know that. They are pouring their money into Africa, and they are not doing that to get us out of poverty. Nobody should be fooled. They know that we are going to squander it all on investments that aren't going to benefit anyone. And because of that, it means we are not creating anything sustainable that would eventually pay off all these Chinese *investments*. Ultimately, we are going to end up with a situation where there are white elephant structures that are not generating income, making it almost impossible for us to pay back the Chinese loans. Essentially the Chinese are enslaving us to generational loans that we will never be able to pay off, while they continue getting all our resources. That is working out exactly the way they planned it. It is not their fault. They are legally exploiting business opportunities. We may argue about the morality of their exploitation behaviour, and that's okay because we are entitled to our opinions, but they are doing nothing wrong. It is our attitude – the African attitude – that is probably morally corrupt.

Before we join the bandwagon and side with the Americans and the Europeans to accuse China for exploiting us, we should look at ourselves first. We must be mature enough to stop this because we know what is happening.

This maturity must extend to personal or individualistic level. If most us cower in our villages, give no toss and have no clue about what our *leaders* negotiate with other nations, then no amount of money is going to help us. It is only Africans who can hold African governments accountable and keep them in check. Unfortunately, we don't care if governments continue with the welfare programs.

Back to Botswana, the country is still experiencing power despite abundance of coal, and there is only 2.3 million of us in Botswana. How is this possible? There is water shortage everywhere including the capital city, which is meant to be the economic hub of the country. Again, how is this possible?

We just can't plan for our future. Has this got anything to do with genetics? A biological deficiency that is disadvantaging us? I am sure science has the answer to this question, but it is too politically incorrect.

To close off this introduction section, let me emphasise that the challenges that blacks in Africa and other none African countries like Jamaica, Papua New Guinea are much different to what blacks in developed nations like USA, Europe, Australia face. What I mean is that in Africa we are in charge. We define our destiny. We control everything. On the other hand, an African-American faces challenges like being in the minority to start with, racism, racial profiling and those kinds of things that we in Africa don't have to worry about. But I am not implying that it is okay for them to be struggling.

* * *

This book is for everyone and not just for Africans, but you will notice that a lot of focus is around the dire situation that we face in Africa. I understand the challenges more and I am speaking or writing from experience and my heart. My hope is that a few people will get the message and act on it. We know about the Bible story of the sower or the Parable of the sower, as it is called. It was a parable told by Jesus, according to the Bible and it goes like:

"A farmer went out to sow his seed. As he was scattering the seed, some fell along the path, and the birds came and ate it up. Some fell on rocky places, where it did not have much soil. It sprang up quickly, because the soil was shallow. But when the sun came up, the plants were scorched, and they withered because they had no root. Other seed fell among thorns, which grew up and choked the plants. **Still other seed fell on good soil, where it produced a crop—a hundred, sixty or thirty times what was sown. Whoever has ears, let them hear***."* – *Matthew 13:1-9*

My hope is that you are the good, fertile "soil" where this seed can grow.

If you are not African, you may have a view about Africa based on what you have read or seen on television. This book would probably give you a truer picture about Africa; a better understanding about our day to day challenges. That way if you want to help, help in any way or form, then you would do so from a better perspective. I am not a big fan of welfare because I know what it does to human beings. It takes away people's ability or willingness to try and fix their problems. I talk about this in one of the chapters in the book.

In Africa, we encourage welfare from household level and all the way to national level. What I mean is that as soon as a family member completes their university studies and starts working, every member of the family breathes a sigh of relief and go to rest because they know that their troubles are over; they look at it is a dawn of a new era. A breadwinner is born, and hunger is gone! That is welfare at its best.

Having said that, I know that sometimes due to life commitments and pressures some people may not have time to go through the trouble of helping Africans by means of ideas, suggestions or education. If that is the case where you feel like the only way you can contribute is by means of donations (cash, clothing, food, etc), then that is still welcome. If you want to donate, go ahead because there are charity organisations out there that are doing wonderful jobs helping those in need in Africa. In that case you can donate, but my focus is around ideas and suggestions on what we can do to get ourselves out of this muddy, slippery mess. The reason I insist on this is because I have laid the argument that just pouring money into Africa is never going to solve our problems. In fact, I believe it is fuelling this situation.

Why are we in this situation in the first place? I will try and cover as much as I can in this book with regards to this question. Unfortunately, I cannot cover all of it because we are not where we are due to just a few errors, but due to many mistakes and errors accumulated over decades or centuries in some cases.

Our errors in judgement started ages ago, including when some Africans sold their fellow Africans to the West as slaves. Why didn't we buy whites as slaves? I wonder. Could it be due to the fact that we are too lazy to lay the foundation for long-term? That our forefathers were more concerned about themselves at that moment and couldn't care less about their future generations? By the way, I am not advocating for slavery. All I am saying if your neighbour is going into business of building something big, did it not cross our minds that we could reverse the trend? Of course not. We are for immediate gratification with no regards for the future.

This book is not going to cover the political aspect of our nightmare. I will touch on that briefly, but I feel like trying to address that here would be a bit of a stretch. My belief is that we must focus our attention on personal growth and development. I think this is more about our attitude than anything else.

In this book, my aim is to try and identify what I believe are the main challenges that are holding us back as Africans and how I think each one of those can be tackled. If you are non-African, you will realise that some of these challenges are general. I believe that for us to be able to solve our challenges we must understand the underlying issues, or the root causes of these problems. The wars, crime, hunger, unemployment, and all that stuff are the symptoms of our deep-rooted challenges.

Obviously, the quick way of getting out of some of the challenges I am going to outline below, is doing the opposite. There is a saying that goes, "to achieve something you have never achieved you must do something you have never done (or be a completely different character)." For us to achieve greatness as Africans, we must do things that we have neither done in the past nor doing today; the opposite of what I define as the challenges.

I will try and explain some of these and the list below is not exhaustive. African challenges are no child's play; they are gigantic and require a gigantic paradigm shift for us to solve. Some of the areas I will cover include:

1. *Laziness – okay, I may be touching a raw nerve here. "How dare you call us lazy," says my fellow African brother or sister. But I insist, most of us (**again, not all**) are too lazy, and I mean full on lazy – indolence is the word. Genetically a lazy race? I don't think so, because there are many hardworking Africans out there. There you go, I said it. I can't take it back and I am sorry for offending you, but most Africans and I can even go as far as most blacks are generally lazy. Not all. I know that the climate we live in is not conducive compared to someone in USA for instance, but we can do better, no question about it. Why didn't we buy whites as slaves? Not that I am suggesting it would have been a good thing, but I'm saying if someone comes in to buy people to go and use them as free labour, why didn't it cross our minds that we could do the same? Well, maybe we were itty-bitty lazy to even do some work with free labour and we didn't want to bother. That is the definition of lazy;*

2. *Poor productivity – ties to the point of laziness above. These two are like bad cousins who are always on sick leave but want to be paid in full at the end of the month. The ones who check their sick leave days and say it's about time I use these days before I will lose*

them. In Africa, it is common to hear a person say, "I am equating effort to money paid." Unbelievable crap if you ask me. You see two men going to replace a door lock and taking hours to do just that and expecting the owner of the house whose lock is being replaced to provide some free coffee or lunch. This my friend, is not a joke, and how I wish it was;

3. Holding grudges – we are very good, or shall I say, bad at that? We don't forget, and we hold grudges on those that were not responsible for events that happened "millions" of years ago responsible for our troubles today, i.e., blaming European settlers and apartheid and all the rest of it for our mediocre lives. It was their grandparents' faults; therefore, they must pay. Someone called it a nigger mentality. Mandela suffered and forgave, why can't we? Are we too special? There is a saying that if you face the sun the shadows will stay behind;

4. Short-sightedness approach – talk about the lack of willingness to do what is necessary today for a better tomorrow. You must have heard about the issue with regards to Cape Town almost running out of drinking water – day zero, that's what it was referred to. Of

course, drought played a role, but government's poor planning and near-sighted approach contributed to this. It is the same across Africa, especially the Sub-Saharan Africa. Botswana does not have enough electricity but abundant coal resources. How can you logically explain that?

5. *Conformance – sticking to the old norms that help no one but the few privileged or the corrupt ones in positions of power. Even as we have access to Internet and the social media, we don't care about learning how the Americans and the Europeans did it. We are happy to maintain the status quo and follow the same old failed path;*

6. *Unwilling to give it shot – why even attempt because others before us have tried and failed? Or who do you think you are, you would be challenged if you dared try. Sadly, a lot of us give up too quickly;*

7. *Urinating on the street – yes, as small as this may sound, it defines us as people. Dirty. A friend of mine studied in Canada for four years. He was studying Bachelor of Science in Mining Engineering and he stayed in Canada for the entire duration of the course and during that four-year period, he never saw a*

person stopping by a tree or a fence and excreting some bodily fluids; the by-product that is urine. After four years, his mental image and philosophy had changed and seeing someone urinating on the street was the last thing in his mind. Well, he landed at the airport and took a taxi to the city. Three minutes into his trip filled with the excitement of meeting his family and friends, he happened to look out the window to enjoy the African view that he hadn't seen in four years. But who could have guessed what would be presented to him on a silver plate? A man in a suit and tie standing in the open urinating and his wife or partner, meters away waiting and chatting to him at the same time. My friend said, he felt like buying a one-way ticket back to Canada! Well, he did not and over time he got used to it;

8. Reading – we do not read. Who has time to read when they are hungry? Africans don't read at all. In fairness, most people in the world do not read. But we read a lot of social media stuff like Facebook feeds and all that rubbish. We also love reading the gossip crap on newspapers. The media people know it and that's what they feed us because it sells. I mentioned Panchu in my acknowledgements earlier; the guy who introduced

me to the multilevel marketing program. Before I met him, I never used to read books. All I was reading was news and I even subscribed to that sh**. It is okay to read news but you don't get better or move ahead in life by reading news about violence, crime, corruption, traffic fines and that sort of stuff. You get ahead by reading about how Sir Richard Branson made it in life or how Mr Strive Musiyiwa started Econet. But, we do not have time for that;

9. Responsibility – blacks, or at least the majority of the black race believe that the problems we find ourselves in are due to someone else. We have to blame others and make them apologise for their deeds, like the former Australian Prime Minister Mr. Kevin Rudd apologised to the Aboriginal people. By the way, I commend him for having the big round balls to do this, but that is sufficient in my eyes. The way forward is upon us, the black community of this planet, to work our way up;

10. Independent or Dependent – You have men and women with their high school aged children living with their parents. It is something that is frowned upon in the West to have someone in their 20s let alone 30s

living with their parents and giving birth and raising their kids at their parents' home. On the other hand, that is common in Africa and we don't seem to be bothered by that;

11. Politics – this is one of those elephants that tends to find a way into a room full of people, creating massive chaos. We have Africans that go around saying, I don't bother about voting because it makes no difference. I say, my friend, start voting because it does make a huge difference. Too many people in Africa are not allowed to vote. So, if you have that rare opportunity to cast your vote please do so. That may be the only way your voice can be heard at the highest level possible. Yes, there is a lot of votes rigging and all that, but if you vote then you expose the cheater and allow for international pressure to be directed at the cheating regime;

12. Attitude – this for me is the single biggest issue of all. In fact, all the topics outlined above point to this one issue – ATTITUDE. This is a broad topic of course, but just working on a few little things can have tremendously positive results in our fortunes. I will talk about this extensively in later chapters. If we

maintain the same attitude, same trajectory or path or whatever we want to call it, then Africa will remain AFRICA (as in what people picture in their minds when you mention Africa – terrible, inhumane, thieves, civil wars, Melbourne's African gangs, jails full of African-Americans, corruption, filthy, and so forth). Africans, and I mean only Africans, can change the fortunes of Africa. No amount of money being pumped in is going to help us until we change our attitude. Accountability. Responsibility. Self-belief;

13. *Education – I am sure you have heard the expression, "everyone is a genius. But if you judge a fish by its ability to climb a tree, it will live its whole life believing that it is stupid." Our education system in Africa does not align to our needs, that is, what skills shortage we need to address. It is about learning the alphabets from A to Z and how to read and write. The other problem is that we are made to believe that you are worth something if you know how to speak English.*

The list is too long but like I said before, I cover what I believe are the main challenges. I am sure there is another book out there where the author outlines what he or she believes are the top priority issues holding us back, but I strongly believe it boils down to the same issues. Exactly what I have touched on above but maybe presented differently. These are the main areas of concern that I believe we must address in our continent to make any significant progress. There is a lot of progress taking place, don't get me wrong, but I think the approach is haphazard and not clearly defined. And if we can address that then I am sure we will see some measurable progress.

We are in so much trouble that for us to get the hell out of that sh** we must start with the basics; the easy action items that we can tick off as completed as quickly as possible. Those things are not going to make us wealthy or rich, but they would mould us to develop better habits. Positive attitude.

As I said, our problems are too many and some are beyond the scope of this book. I cannot help the situation in South Sudan for instance. But what we can do is improve what is around the South Sudanese. What I mean is that if what is around you is better and beautiful then you are likely to follow suit. A thief living amongst decent and honourable people is likely to leave his or her thieving ways behind. Otherwise, they wouldn't fit in. Similarly, if what surrounds

South Sudan is progress then chances are that this culture of progress would eventually cross the border.

Some of the things I talk about are so basic that someone in the first world would wonder and go, *really?*

Finally, when you get a chance please visit my website http://www.makeafricabetter.info/blog and leave a comment or some advice that you believe can go a long way in helping us in Africa. We need all the help we can get. This book alone is not going to solve our problems and in fact that's not what I am trying to do. What I am doing here is to start a debate and some form of discussion where we can have civil disagreements and suggestions that can empower us to rise above our challenges. It is possible, but it is going to take some time and effort.

Some Context and Numbers

There are multiple sources to these numbers but a quick search on the internet reveals similar results:

- 16 out of the 20 poorest countries (where people live on less than $1,000 per year) are in Africa. South Sudan is the worst at $246 per year (or $0.67 per day);

- 11 of the 20 most corrupt countries are in Africa, with the majority in the Sub-Saharan Africa region;

- 19 out of 20 countries with the lowest life expectancy are in Africa. Afghanistan is the only non-African country on that list;

14. This is not a book about World Bank and World Health Organisation statistics, but maybe just knowing this information would make you appreciate our challenges.

CHAPTER 1 – Education

"Knowledge is power. Information is liberating. Education is the premise of progress, in every society, in every family."
~ Kofi Annan

Our parents used to say (and I am literally translating from Setswana – a Botswana native language – to English), *if you don't go to school you'll eat your mates' dirt.* In fact, they used a derogatory word instead of *dirt*. Simply put, if you play around or skip classes when your age mates are busy studying and working hard to get good grades at school, chances are that you will end up working for them in future either as their subordinate or as a servant (cleaning their houses, hence their dirt). This was true then, true today and will forever be true. I am sure you've experienced it once in your lifetime, where you met your former school mate who is going through some difficult moments in his or her life – struggling to make ends meet. Sometimes you can't help but feel sorry and remember how playful the person was at school when they still had a chance. That is all too common in rural Africa.

The lack of education or the low percentage of kids attending school is probably the most challenging huddle that is slowing Africa's progress. It is terribly hard to make much progress in life without the ability to read and write. We have many school-aged kids roaming the streets doing nothing of value for themselves nor the society they live in. The end-product is delinquent youths terrorising villagers and others getting into substance abuse. Those who don't stray into delinquency are usually *abused* to work as herd boys and girls. I call it *abuse* because that is one form of child labour and it doesn't get much airtime because the abuse is usually perpetrated by their parents or close relatives.

It is a vicious cycle where these kids grow up to become parents and since they never went to school, education is not considered a must for their children. When there is no pressure from parents to go to school, no child is going to move mountains to force their way to school. Because, let's face it, who likes going to school? During my school days, there was never a day where I woke up in the morning and grinned when the thought of my class teacher crossed my mind. I frowned and just hated the fact that the night ended. It felt like all my weekdays nights were too short, and the school days were excruciatingly long. For most days, going to school meant one thing – unnecessary punishment in the name of discipline. The so-called discipline dished out against African children can be severe; caning or lashes on one's backside. Now, imagine going to school with a heavy heart, while your mates (kids whose parents don't give a toss about school) are playing football on the street not bothered about going to school. It was a terrible feeling and that tempted others to skip school. I must admit that I was a "victim" where I would leave home in the morning pretending that I was off to school, then hid in the bushes and when school ended I would go back home as if I had been to school all day. Thankfully my grandmother straightened me up before it was too late. Unfortunately, others are not so lucky.

Another major obstacle is the fact that in some areas, kids have to travel long distances to get to school. When I started school, we walked about 7 km one way to get to school and this went on for 4 years of my primary education. By the time we got to school, we would be tired and the last thing we needed when tired was to listen to some boring math lesson. The exhaustion and the discomfort of the sitting arrangement where we sat on the ground under trees made it too hard to concentrate. Food was provided at school, but it was only at 11 a.m. and that made the first half of the day impossible to focus.

These unfavourable conditions lead to a lot of kids dropping off school altogether. If the parents don't see the importance of school, the desire to stay home outweighed the need to go to school. So, the majority didn't (and even today don't) bother.

Without basic education, especially from grades 1 to 12, it is a tall order to succeed in life and the evidence is in every rural village in Africa. The level of poverty is heartbreaking. It is impossible to make serious headways in terms of human development without education and hard for Africa to keep up the pace with the rest of the world. Until we address this issue our chances of sitting around a negotiation table with the Chinese or the Americans as equal partners will be too slim. These countries will forever have an upper hand when negotiating trade deals with us.

When a child and eventually an adult misses the foundation bit, years 1 to 12, it makes it tough for them to grasp other important life lessons post formal education – politics (especially politics in Africa) and finance. I think these are the 2 most important lessons that Africans must learn if we are to achieve prosperity for our continent.

Non-streamlined Education

I found the above image online and I thought, *wow, what an excellent depiction of our education system!* I mentioned before that we all need the foundation for us to understand the basics of politics and finances, for instances. Mind you, I chose these two topics (politics and finance) because I believe they are our major areas of weakness. Poverty for instance, has got a lot to do with politics and finances. Rampant corruption is the same – the love of money and political influence. Civil wars are political and have a lot to do with money too. Elections rigging, the same story. That is how I decided on these two. There is a section on politics in the next few pages.

Earlier I outlined some of the obstacles discouraging African children to attend school. Unfortunately, for those who manage to navigate these obstacles, the standard of education offered is the one-size-fits-all type. Good education must have the end in mind. In other words, it must be aligned to the needs of the continent. At the moment it is the same for everyone with no regards to our future needs. Not only that, but the majority of those fortunate enough to go all the way to tertiary level leave school ill-equipped to face life challenges head-on. Back to my two important topics, most graduate enter the labour force with zero knowledge about the politics in their country let alone the rest of the continent.

I am no exception to this by the way. I only started developing interest in these topics very late into my adult life. I felt that I had an engineering degree, a well-paying job and I did not care. That is a disease that most Africans suffer. It is all down to the one-size-fits-all approach.

Our education system needs a complete overhaul. There has to be some form of training where African high school students do courses around the following:

- African challenges;

- How Mr Robert Mugabe messed up the Zimbabwean economy (basically the what-not-to-do type of learning and Mugabe happened to be an easy target for me in this case). The late Jim Rohn used to talk about how he wished unsuccessful people could give talks or do workshops about how they miscalculated as far as making life decisions go;

- About politics and making sure people understand that their voices are powerful and can be used for the good of their countries;

- Talk about how successful people like Dr Patrice Motsepe succeeded, or where possible the training should pick some successful individuals and present their complete biography. Ideally these must be people who started from humble beginnings and they don't have to be wealthy people. It could be people who are doing well in their careers after tough starts;

- American success stories, why they are ahead of us and how they raise their kids to be independent at a younger age. It could be any country for that matter.

- I strongly believe that we need courses along these lines to enhance our knowledge about life challenges in general. Currently, when we complete our studies and start working, it becomes trial and error all the

, and by the time we "wake up" and grasp the basics about life, it is almost too late in our lives.

- The current education system is neither tailor made to meet our continent's needs nor aligned to students' capabilities. It is a template copied from the West (our masters) and imposed on Africans. For instance, the Botswana system is aligned to the British system mainly because we were colonised by the British. At the start of the book I shared the quote, "everyone is a genius. But if you judge a fish by its ability to climb a tree, it will live its whole life believing that it is stupid." We are all different and our education syllabuses must align to that reality. I know that I am talking about Africa as though it is one large country, which it is not. But, the challenges are the same especially for Sub-Saharan Africa.

What can be done?

- All life challenges can be solved including these seemingly insurmountable challenges. With education, it would take time. A good start would be for our governments to revamp our education system. A complete overhaul to address the limitations I addressed above.

- In the absence of this overhaul, I believe parents can help too. I am talking about parents who have some knowledge about what is happening. One of the things that I have personally started doing is get my first-born daughter some self-development books to read as presents. It requires some encouragement and motivation, but it has to be done. Knowledge is the key. Remember that sometimes all it takes is turning that one stone at a time. Even you as you read this book, I believe you will take it upon yourself to impair knowledge into your children, loved ones and friends.

- The media can play a very important role as well in spreading this education message. The print media could dedicate a page where they cover educational stuff. These could be in a form of entertaining short stories. It is even easier these days with social media because some of these things can be shared easily.

Politics

You: Theo, have you registered to vote?

Theo: I don't vote, it is waste of time.

You: Why do you think that?

Theo: It makes no difference. Politicians never do what they promise us.

You: Yeah, but that's the more reason you have to vote. That is probably the only way you can have your voice heard.

- This is another area that requires serious attention and it feeds into the education narrative as I mentioned before. People in the Western world use politics to shape their future – for better or for worse. Depending on when you read this book, the current situation (2019) in the UK with regards to Brexit is something that came about due to politics. People voted to leave the European Block. You can argue for or against, but people used the power of one man one vote (or to be politically correct, one person one vote). President Donald J Trump is another example of people using the power of a vote to decide the future of their country. A lot of people despised Hillary Clinton and the mention of her name and her not-so-favourable past led to people to go and vote against her. Not taking anything away from President Trump, but the general sentiment was that "I would rather have Trump than Clinton" and they prevailed. That is the power of politics.

- Obviously, it is a lot more complicated in Africa than in America or Britain. We still have a lot of corruption and votes rigging. Staying away due to electoral fraud is not going to help though. People must be taught and made to understand the importance of voting. As more people vote against the government, for instance, it gets to a point where it gets harder for the electoral commission to rig. The sheer volume would make it harder to rig the elections.

- But, this will only work if people understand what's in it for them. The onus is on us, the so-called learned (or educated?), to impart the knowledge on the less educated. Ordinary Africans don't usually differentiate between policy and party. I know that parties tend to align to policies, but we have instances where a politician can have certain views about issues that don't necessarily align to his or her political party and in that case people must vote based on policy not party lines.

Reading

"A person who won't read has no advantage over one who can't read."
~ *Mark Twain*

One of the things that I used to hate was getting a self-help book and reading. I believed that with my education, my degree, I was smart enough and there wasn't anything that anyone could teach me about life. I can tell you that this was my single biggest mistake by a mile. I made a lot of mistakes in my lifetime but the failure to read was the worst, without a shadow of a doubt.

A lot of us believe that getting a certificate is a major achievement (and it is) and marks the end of your learning. The truth is that that piece of paper, your certificate, just defines the finish line for formal education and the beginning of life lessons. If you think that your certificate is the end of your learning period then you are not matured, just like I was for a long time. Your life is probably going to be unfulfilling.

There is no way of putting this any simpler. The bottom line is:

> *We must read self-help books.*

Most of these books contain rich information and the beautiful thing about these books is that most of the stuff covered are real-life stories or what the author learnt in his or her lifetime. A book can save you years of trial and error exercises; the so-called reinventing the wheel. You may find that the book is a true reflection of your life or close to it. Books are richer than *gold and diamond* and as far as personal development is concerned, they are a good start because you can read a book in the comfort of your bed or a stool under a tree.

Some of the great books that I have read include:

- Think and Grow Rich by Napoleon Hill
- The 7 Habits of Highly Effective People by Stephen Covey
- The Richest Man in Babylon by George Samuel Clason
- The Magic of Thinking Big by David J. Schwartz
- Eat that Frog by Brian Tracy

And many others but I believe these are some of the best books that you can read for your personal development.

I appreciate that we have high illiteracy levels in Africa, but we have to start somewhere. The ones who were fortunate enough to get that formal education must continue learning beyond the walls of educational institutions; self-help and personal development is the way to go. We cannot continue pumping graduates after graduates onto the African streets who know nothing beyond their school qualifications.

I never used to read these self-help books until someone introduced me to Network Marketing (Mr. and Mrs. Panchu – see acknowledgment section). I am neither endorsing nor discouraging you to join these programs, but I am just telling you that that is where I got introduced to reading these types of books. As I started reading these books my perception of life changed for the better. I was too negative and never accepted responsibility on most mistakes I made. And the more I read these books, the more mature I became. I started being happier than before (I was almost always in a crappy mood and I was referred to as a short-tempered person with a short fuse or too sensitive. I probably still am but I have control over my anger issues now).

Many years ago when I was in high school, I used to read fiction novels (the so-called Pacesetter Novels). These types of books are just like going to the movie theatre to watch a love story movie. They are enjoyable fantasy stories, but you don't learn much or anything out of them at all. There is nothing wrong with watching a fantasy movie or reading a fiction novel, I am just trying to show you that your time could be spent well somewhere else and that's with the personal development books.

If you want to grow as a person, I kindly urge you to spend a few bucks to purchase yourself a book. Just spend time to read self or personal development books (and it doesn't have to be any of the above books), but anything about your development. I don't believe there is any human challenge today that has not been discussed thoroughly in a form of a book along with resolutions for those challenges. I can bet my last dollar and tell you that whatever challenge you have today, someone somewhere on this planet has written a book or done a research on that challenge. The challenge is having the desire to go out and finding that solution; looking for that book or a document outlining these issues.

Audios or Videos

This is another platform that you can use for your personal development and this is good if you are not keen on reading. Like in my case, I enjoy listening to the late Jim Rohn via audio recordings or YouTube videos. The good thing about audios (compared to books) is that you can listen while driving. Someone once said it is like being in a mobile library where you learn as you drive. Most of these videos and audios are not too long – usually 1 hour to 2 hours – and if you are taking a long trip you can get a couple or so done in one hit.

There are thousands of these videos and audios online and most of them a free. Authentic and free – how often can you have these two words in one sentence in this age of fake news? But, yes there are thousands of informative recordings online, especially YouTube. My favourite ones include Jim Rohn, Brian Tracy, Les Brown, just to name a few. There are many others and you want to listen to something that inspires you; gets you moving. So, my preferred speakers may not necessarily be your bread-and-butter type.

Note that you can only come across these people by associating with the right people, who can in turn introduce you to these types of things. For me it all started when I joined the network marketing team. As noted earlier, they introduced me to books, audios, talking to people and I did not like either one of these things.

I thought this was funny and you can skip if you want. Someone once wrote that,

> "*The African education system is such that the smartest students become doctors and engineers. The second string do MBAs and LLBs, therefore manage the smartest. The third string become politicians and rule, not lead but rule, the above. The failures go into the military and police services where they control the politicians, and hence all the above. Those who never went to school become prophets and we all follow them.*"

Maybe a bit of an exaggeration but there is some truth to this.

CHAPTER 2 – The Life Choices

"It's not what happens in the world that determines the major part of your future. What happens, happens to us all. The key is what you do about it."
~ Mr. Jim Rohn

"We are where we are and what we are because of the choices and decisions that we have made in the past."
~ Brian Tracy

How do you define life? It is said that life is like a jigsaw puzzle with thousands, millions even, of small and large pieces that we should put together into a picture that makes sense. Each piece has a place on the jigsaw board. One wrong move can set you back years. For as long as you live, you shall play this game, moving these puzzle pieces to their rightful place on the jigsaw board. And this is going to be every day of your life without fail and if you stop playing you fall behind.

The moves you make are your daily life CHOICES. I am not sure about you, but most people play games with the sole intention of winning. That applies to all the games including this puzzle that is life.

I, like most people make my life choices with the belief that they (the choices I make) will enhance my quality of life and for those closest to me; my family and friends. But occasionally we stray off course (place that puzzle piece at or on a wrong spot) but when that happens the ideal thing to do is to correct course. We make these life choices with the best intentions. Sometimes we don't even realise that we made a bad move. And if nobody brings that to our attention or we don't learn from those mistakes, then that's it. We are screwed. How do you get told that you've made a bad move? There are lots of ways and it could be:

- A friend or a spouse telling you,
- Maybe you learn by reading a book,
- It could be through a training course,
- Or a workshop/conference.

As we move these pieces of our life puzzle, we define our future. In most cases, the moves we make are very small. Please note that:

Small life choices do not equate to inconsequential outcomes.

Sometimes the choices we make can be the difference between life and death. Before going too far into this chapter, I am going to tell you a real-life story about a life choice that turned out to be the last choice that one of my schoolmates ever had to make in his life. Please note that this is not in any way meant to be disrespectful or ridicule this late guy, his family or people that were affected by this incident (a life choice). There may be some minor inaccuracies too because this happened over 25 years ago in 1993 and based on what I was told at the time, but the message is true. This will set the tone for the rest of this chapter relating to choices:

> *This happened a year after I completed my high school, which was a boarding school where maybe half the student population stayed on school premises. We were provided with everything, food, water, electricity, beds, all the facilities. During my last year at that school we had a riot where we complained about the quality of food. It was so bad that it led to broken windows, damaged school property, personal property like teachers' cars, you name it. We just went berserk, you know, just going bananas. Can you imagine? Almost everything was provided at no cost to us. Free education. Free food. Free tea or coffee. Free cold drinks. All we had to bring were*

our clothing and bedding items like sheets, blankets and pillows as well as our toiletry.

Anyway, as you may already know, if you stay at a boarding school it means you must follow the school's code of conduct. These were nothing major and the main one being that we were not allowed to leave school campus without permission, and this happened to be the code or rule that was violated the most. 'We are not prisoners,' we would reason.

After school hours, we were under some form of supervision by someone referred to as the Boarding Master. All he did was make rounds at certain times to make sure that the beds were not empty, but it was not easy monitoring hundreds of students. At high school level especially towards the end (yr 11 and 12) a lot of students feel like they are grownups and start engaging in stuff like alcohol, relationships etc., all of which were not allowed on campus.

People usually like the forbidden stuff, we know this from the beginning of time; the Adam and Eve story about the forbidden fruit.

Even though alcohol was not allowed the students had a way of accessing it. (This is a choice by the way, where someone decides that 'alcohol is not allowed but I will find a way to get it.') The busiest time for the boarding master was weekends because the boarding boys and girls would normally jump the school fence and head into the village night clubs for entertainment and that meant booze.

But one of those weekends turned out to be the last for one for one of the students (Tshepho* - not his real name). The night (Saturday) started well with diner at the school hall. The usual nice, free food that students did not appreciate at all. Anyway, after diner the routine included going back to the rooms (hostels) for a short break and then at around 7 p.m. it was party time; record night, it was called. Basically, the chairs and tables in the school's dining hall were moved out of the way, leaving a large open dance floor turning the place into a night club. We would dance and party until about midnight, alcohol free of course.

It was during this time that a lot of students would sneak out, jump the fence and go to the village night clubs. The disco nights made it hard for the boarding master to monitor who was in or out and the students exploited that opportunity.

On one of those record nights, the boys jumped the fence and headed to the village. When the boys got to the village night club/bar they started drinking and one of the boys from school Mmoloki (not his real name) got involved in a fight with one of the boys from the village (we will call him Tebogo).

The fight ended or at least that was what Mmoloki thought because he had beaten Tebogo. They got back to partying because they had limited time. They had to be back at school before the end of the record night. Meanwhile, Tebogo had other ideas; apparently he organised a knife and when he got back with that knife, he mistook Tshepho for Mmoloki. Sadly, Tshepho was killed in the event.

This is a true story, unfortunately, except the names. Again, no disrespect intended, and I apologise for the offence and pain that this may cause.

Sadly, this was a life choice. Choosing to jump the fence is not a big life choice in the grand scheme of things because the worst that could happen, as far as punishments go, was to get caught, be summoned to the principal's office, receive two lashes each on their backside and that would be it; done and dusted. And the sequence would be repeated the following weekend, and the one following that and so forth until graduating from the high school.

Getting a couple of lashes was regarded as a small price to pay for the weekend filled with booze and girls or boys out in the village. Students jumped the fence every weekend and nothing ever happened.

This is not meant to judge those poor souls, we know that students usually do all kinds of things especially at that age. We all did. It is just that some of us live to look back and maybe laugh about what we did, and other times it can be life-changing. It is what is referred to as short term gratification with no consideration for the bigger picture and long-term consequences.

You can only imagine the impact this act had on the lives of his friends. What started off as a quick dash to the night club turned into a nightmare.

Consider the following small choice that I made when I was younger:

One time as I was walking home from school, maybe 13 years old at the time, I had a sudden urge to use the toilet. A day earlier I had a large tree thorn pierce my right foot heel, causing severe swelling, so I was limping. We had no shoes during those days. Anyway, as I was walking I realised that I wasn't going to make it out to the bush (yes, the bush was our toilet) because I was walking too slow due to the swollen heel. Just a few metres ahead I saw a goats' kraal in the middle of the village and that got me thinking and before I knew it I was inside the kraal. I paused, looked around; left, right and behind, I didn't see anyone. I was like a night thief in the middle of the day. Right in the middle of my act the owners' boys, probably 2 school grades older, saw me and all hell broke loose. They started chasing me with their dogs. I have no idea how I got out of that kraal, but I know it wasn't though the entrance. I was in a flight mode, the catch-me-if-you-can type. I ran so fast that there was even some dust behind me, dogs barking, with some disturbing profanity directed at me. They never caught up. I was a bullet.

I don't think anyone would consider this a significant life choice. At worst, it was embarrassing at the time and that is the point. I made a choice to enter that kraal to answer nature's call. It is something that I can look back at and laugh about. It is true that small life choices may lead to little or no impact in our lives and this was one of those.

Again, consider another situation where you are working for a company and you are always a couple of minutes late for meetings. A couple or 2 minutes late is a relatively small time lost, but the significance is huge, and people will judge you unfavourably for this *small,* 2-minutes act.

The examples above were meant to highlight the point I made earlier about "small" life choices. That is, small life choices do not equate to inconsequential outcomes.

Whatever choice or life decision you make has some form of consequences in future.

Your current life choices define your future

"Life is about choices. Some we regret, some we're proud of. Some will haunt us forever. The message: we are what we chose to be."
~ Graham Brown

A great philosopher once said that wherever you are in life today, is a result of the thousands or even millions of choices you made in the past.

Chances are that sometime in the past you got to a crossroad situation, pondered about the direction to follow and eventually chose what seemed like the best option at the time. Other people take their time to choose their options but some of us just rush in and think afterwards. The latter is what most of us do, especially in Africa. We tend to go with the option of *act and think afterwards* and that is very bad.

Other decisions are not so crossroad-type. The instinctive type where you just act. There is nothing wrong with that. It is human. It is natural.

There is a lot of suffering of in Africa and most of it is down to our life choices. The conditions are not the best for most people in our continent. It is a lot harder. I understand that. Life is not easy. It was never meant to be. That is why it is important that we make the right choices.

The problem is that if you were to ask around someone would tell you that it was someone else's fault that they are suffering. We always blame it on someone, not our life choices. We will discuss the issue of BLAME in the next chapter because it ties in well with the issue of CHOICE.

If you feel like the entire universe and everything on it is pulling against you, then don't despair. I know a lot of people feel that way. I felt that way for a long time. Do not despair, I say; consider yourself fortunate because at least you made a choice to read a book like this one. It is not all lost and maybe reading this book will be one of those choices that will change your life. Let this be a turning point in your life.

As I said earlier, the decisions we made in the past shaped our current state of affairs. The choices we are making today are going to shape our future.

You may say that is not true or that you had bad advice or whatever, and so forth. It doesn't matter but I am telling you the truth. All those choices you made in the past are the reason you are in your current situation – good or bad. Whether you made these choices consciously or subconsciously, it still doesn't matter. What matters are your actions. By actions I mean the decisions (CHOICES) you made.

Remember that it is not always about the magnitude of the action you took at the time. It is true that sometimes the small choices you made did not have an impact on their own at the time, but the accumulation of those small choices over time can have devastating effects – and longevity usually leads to that.

It is like gaining weight over a long period by eating just an extra 50 calories more than you need every day. Someone may say it is only 50 calories, but those 50s add up over time. If you were to check your weight daily I can guarantee you that you would go days without noticing any weight increase. But that doesn't mean that you are not accumulating fat. It is piling up slowly.

If you are in high school (or secondary school) just be mindful that the choices you are making today will define your future. And I would say you are one fortunate student in that you got an opportunity to read a book like this while you still at that level. You have time on your side. A lot of people are not so fortunate to get this type of knowledge at your age. Don't even think for a second that your decisions at that age don't matter. In fact, at that age, that is where you are busy consolidating habits that will define your character as a mature human being.

If you are older, again you are lucky to be reading this book because you still have time to turn your life around if it didn't turn out to be what you wanted. It is just that someone in high school has a lot more time on their side to plan. It is always easier to make mistakes and recover from those errors in judgement when you are younger with less commitments like family and those unplanned bank loans. When you are 50 years old (with school-going kids, that bank personal loan, mortgage, car loan, etc.) it can be a daunting task; not impossible, just a little harder. But the great thing is that sometimes you need only about 6 – 8 years to be debt-free, for instance. With that in mind, be positive and rid yourself of those negative thoughts about your age. You have plenty of time to make a difference in your life.

We shape and choose our futures. It does not happen by mistake or chance. To be a doctor, you've got to choose to be a doctor many years prior to being one. Just stating the obvious, going to a medical school is one of those choices that must be made before becoming a doctor.

It is the same as being involved in crime. It's not like it just happens overnight where you go *today I am going to rob a bank*. It is one of those where you potentially chose to associate with the wrong mob and ended up getting involved in making bad decisions.

I am sorry to keep repeating this over and over, but we are where we are based on our life choices. This is a universal law, if you will, and it is applicable to our parents and their parents and many generations well before them.

Consider this fascinating story that I believe will resonate well with this principle of choice. Maybe you've heard this story before but that's still fine because it does not hurt to go over something again just to reflect. I have used fake names to help with the narration.

> *The story is about a family that lived in a small, beautiful village called Tsiokoro in Western Botswana. It is said that there lived a family of four; husband, wife and their two children. The husband's name was Jakoba, and his wife's name was Malebogo and they had lovely identical twin sons, Kaine and Abele. No, not the famous "Cain and Abel" from the book of Genesis.*
>
> *The family was impoverished and struggled to make ends meet. Unemployment was high and a lot of people resorted to spending their days sitting under tree shades, counting every minute of their days with no hope in sight; an unfortunate situation which is common place in Africa, especially the Sub Sahara part of this wonderful continent.*

Anyway, Jakoba and Malebogo resorted to drinking alcohol to try and forget their problems. The drinking got so bad that they would drink and sleep where they last drank. They would just blackout and sleep right there.

Anyway, without going into too much detail, after many years when Kaine and Abele were grown up men, living separate lives away from their home village, their father died of old age. During the funeral the pastor, Pastor Enoke, who was leading the proceedings for the funeral could not help but notice the contrast between Kaine and Abele. The difference in their lifestyle and behaviour was as pronounced as black and white. Just two extreme opposites. The pastor thought to himself that he would like to talk to the twins separately after the funeral just to understand the difference in their lifestyles.

As he had promised himself earlier, Pastor Enoke had just one simple question for the twins and separately he asked them "Why did your life turn out this way?" Kaine's response was a rumbling, defensive, and maybe even a disrespectful answer. He resented the pastor for even asking responding, "Enoke (not even referring to him as Pastor Enoke), how could you even ask such a stupid question?"

He went on to explain that there was no way he could have made it in life given how his parents drank and that the odds were stacked heavily against him. He just grew up to be like his father. As is the norm in our African traditions, the pastor was kind of 'understanding' and sympathetic when he heard Kaine's story. It made complete sense to him and he even promised to pray for him.

Well his views were shattered when he heard Abele's answer moments later. It was one of those well-I-never-thought-about-that type moments where you go, 'hmm, interesting,' because Abele's response was swift and telling. It left the priest scratching his head and gently caressing his long unkempt grey beard.

"I didn't want to be like my father" was all that Abele said.

It is what you do going forward that matters. For the preceding story, *Kaine and Abele made some big life choices!* Abele took charge of his life and Kaine did not.

There were multiple similarities for these boys from the beginning; the same birth place, they were identical twins, they grew up under the same conditions, but we end up with two adult twins, two completely different outcomes on their perspective about life. Why is that? Well, remember the quote at the start of this chapter, *"it's not what happens in the world that determines the major part of your future. What happens, happens to us all. The key is what you do about it."*

Same circumstance all the way to adulthood but different choices in the end. The reason I am telling this story is that it is very common in Africa to find people in a similar situation like Kaine. People who believe it is impossible to achieve anything of worth in their lives because of how hopeless the situation is. Don't get me wrong here. I believe it is harder for Africans compared any other race on earth. This is not an exaggeration and nor an excuse. Africa is not for the fainthearted. It is tough. We have to make serious sacrifices and choices to get out of our current situation.

The good thing about the human species is that we have the benefit of making decisions that define our destiny. We are the only creation that can stop, reflect and say *today is the day, I am changing course because I am tired of this life of mediocrity, I want to leave a great legacy behind when I depart this planet*. I am not saying it is easy but it is possible.

Choose GOOD over BAD

Make the right choices today or pay a heavy price tomorrow. Unfortunately, some of us live the rest of our lives haunted by the bad choices we made in the past. It is not worth it. That is how I lived my life for a long time. Let me emphasise my theme and that is, these choices don't have to be classified as high impact. What matters is that if they are repeated over and over for a long period of time you may find yourself completely off course by thousands of miles. I like the analogy by M. J. DeMarco in his book – The Millionaire Fastlane: Crack the Code to Wealth and Live Rich for a Lifetime – where he compares small mistakes to a golf ball trajectory path. He says:

> *When the clubface hits the ball square, the ball goes straight and heads toward the hole. But when the clubface is rotated a fraction of one degree, the ball's trajectory lands far off course. At impact, the divergence is minor, but as the ball travels further it widens and widens until the gap is so large that getting back on track is nearly impossible. A bad choice can set your trajectory off by only one degree today, but over years the error is magnified.*

The problem is that we underestimate the impact our "small" choices have on our lives. If you are in high school and fortunate enough to read this book, I plead to you that you analyse your choices. Who are your friends? Are they the type that would lead you in the right direction? Remember that at that stage in your life, it is usually those you associate with that have a major influence on your life; this is when you are still developing and building those habits. Below is a true story about my cousin, who had his life and character shaped while at high school.

> *My cousin and I stayed together in a small hut when we were in high school (if you didn't know, a hut is* **a small, simple, single-storey house or shelter** *– Dictionary. African huts are built from mud, wood/logs and grass). The boys he associated with were bad; they drank alcohol, were forever chasing girls, fighting, and all those stupid stuff young boys do. Fortunately for me, him and I were just like water and oil. We just didn't connect. For him it was just unfortunate because that behaviour and his company at that age shaped his character into adulthood.*
>
> *Years later, in his early 30s he was undone by these wrong choices. He dated a woman, who happened to*

have a 15-year old daughter (and nothing wrong with that I must state). His downfall was that he got attracted to the daughter and they started dating. He started shunning the girl's mother, and that broke her heart. She suspected that my cousin was seeing someone, but her daughter was the last person she suspected. When the truth finally came out where she knew whom my cousin was going out with, she lost it. It was bad enough for him to break her heart and cheat, but to do so with her own daughter, under the same roof, a room just meters away was a red line that couldn't be crossed. It was completely unacceptable in her life and she was out for my cousin's blood. He had to pay.

Long story short, my cousin was ultimately sentenced to 15 years in prison for sleeping with an underage girl. Sadly, he lost his life on his third year of incarceration.

I am not trying to be the judge here. Just laying out the facts. My cousin's habits were shaped while he was still at high school. At the time these didn't seem like anything major. He was dating girls and big deal. But that shaped his future.

Let me repeat that if you are lucky enough to be reading this book, whether in high school, university, college or whatever stage you are at in your life, just think about the long-term consequences of the choices you are making today. Choose right. Choose life.

I believe this is probably the most important piece of the puzzle (the life puzzle). CHOICES. LIFE CHOICES. Africa and all of us the African people are where we are today because of the choices we made and continue to make. It does not require a *rocket scientist* to tell anyone that those choices were or are bad. Just drive to a remote African village in Mozambique or any African country and you will understand what I am talking about. It cannot be explained any other way. We are poor because of the collective choices we make as African citizens.

Remember that it is pointless to try to reason about what you did in the past. The important thing is to take stock of your life, look at the CHOICES you made and if the path you are on is not leading you to *the promised land of milk and honey* then it is probably ideal to change direction. Maintaining the same path would be naive and no one is going to listen to you if you try to reason your failures. Your opinion would be referred to as *moo opinion* (I know!).

A *moo point* was a phrase from a USA television sitcom show called *Friends* that ran on NBC. In one of the scenes, one of the characters, Rachel was trying to source an opinion from the other characters on the show in relation to her recent breakup with her boyfriend. Then Joey, another character on the show asked Rachel whether their opinion mattered, that is, would it mean much to the boyfriend (or former boyfriend). Joey went on to say if their reasoning did not matter then it would all be like a *moo point* and below is how the conversation went:

> **Joey**: All right, Rach. The big question is, "does he like you?" All right? Because if he doesn't like you, this is all a moo point.
> **Rachel**: Huh. A moo point?
> **Joey**: Yeah, it's like a cow's opinion. It just doesn't matter. It's moo.

Now this is where I am saying if your life is in chaos do not attempt to explain or reason to others because it would all come down to *it doesn't matter.* It would be a classic case of a *cow's opinion*.

Corruption

Fighting corruption is not just good governance. It's self-defense. It's patriotism.
~Joe Biden

Africa is where it is today because of the devastating choices that our political leaders (maybe political rulers is more appropriate) made in the past and continue making even to this day. Some of the decisions make you wonder if there is any shame in it or not. Like President of Equatorial Guinea, Teodoro Obiang Nguema promoting his son Teodorin Nguema Obiang to the position of Vice President. This happened in 2016. How can this be acceptable? What impact do you think this would have to the future of the country? Not positive.

Corruption is a life choice that a lot of Africans make all the time. I am not even talking about corruption associated with political rulers, which is usually reported in newspapers including in the West. I am talking about the one at departmental levels that goes under the radar like a contractor administrator awarding small contracts and projects to his or her relatives, friends or those who pay some commission to get the jobs. This is probably the worst because the jobs I am referring to are those that affect our day to day lives like installing sewage systems, connecting water pipes, building a few houses for teachers. These are projects occurring across Africa and their impact on people's lives is huge. The projects are never delivered on time because they were awarded to incompetent friends and the worst part is that they usually cost more.

Africa is where it is because we choose to be silent when all these issues take place right in front of us. It is even bad when people tell you that you think you are better when you raise some of these issues. Patriotism is making noise about these issues.

Botswana is ranked one of the least corrupt countries in the world. That is a very good accomplishment. Personally, I am challenging this as false. We just happen to be one of the most peaceful countries in Africa and my theory is that we are not drawing too much attention to ourselves. If you were to ask someone in a developed country if they have ever heard of a country called Botswana, chances are that they would say negative. It is good in a sense because we are peaceful and politically stable, but those in power exploit this because nobody is really *watching* us all the time. A lot of corruption goes unnoticed.

And as soon as you try and bring this to people's attention you get *but we are the least corrupt in Africa.* It is commendable but we should never accept any level of corruption. Remember that that tolerance adds up and before you know it the entire society is corrupt. It becomes a norm and acceptable.

These are terrible life choices and must be dealt with accordingly.

Understood, So what's next?

Based on the information I shared for this chapter, the key is for us to reflect on where we are today and take stock. We cannot change what happened in the past, but we can define the course of our future just like Abele did in the story of Kaine and Abele. Following the same path and pretending that everything is going to be okay guarantees us one thing and that is, we would be talking about the same issues 100 years later. We have to change. That's all it is.

If you stay silent even when you see corruption, then you are guilty. Silence means consent. In today's world there are so many avenues to make your voice heard, including social media. Say something and someone would hear you.

Chapter 2 Summary

- Are the choices you make on daily basis the kind of stuff you wouldn't mind seeing on the front page of the local newspaper? Not embarrassing? If so, maybe you are on the right track. Anytime you do something that you don't feel comfortable seeing splashed on the front page of the newspaper then maybe it is not right.

- Your choices define you. You are a product of your past decisions. Ten years down the line your life would be a mirror reflection of the choices you made today. The exciting thing is that you are a human being. The exciting thing about being human is that you can decide today and make a 180-degree change in direction and follow a different path.

- Remember that it is never too late. Whatever you age is, you are probably going to live another 20, 30 or so years. Imagine if you are 60 years old and saying "it is too late, I am old. Only if I was still in my twenties or thirties!" What if you still have another 30 – 35 years to live? How about live those years comfortably? It is never too late. Even if you have a few years to live, how about leaving a positive legacy for your loved ones? You may not be able to accumulate millions of dollars for the time left but you can share knowledge that can shape the future of those closest to you for the rest of their lives in a positive way. Share your mistakes and advice your future generation not to follow the same path. Our problem in Africa is that sometimes we care about ourselves only and worry less about the future that doesn't include us. That is a shame. That must change.

- It is not about the size or magnitude of the choice you make that matters. What matters is the fact that it is a bad choice that nudges you off course a little bit but due to longevity, you may end way off course. Remember that example about hitting a golf ball a fraction off the right direction? It is similar to eating an extra 50 calories over the required amount. In theory, over 30 years this translates to 30 years x 366 days/year x 50 calories/day = 549,000 calories! It is estimated that 3,500 calories are equal to about 1 pound (~450 grams) of fat and based on this theory it means over a 30-year period you would have accumulated 549,000 calories divide by 3,500 calories per 450g of fat, which translates to about 70,586 grams of fat (or 70.6 kg of excess fat!). Obviously, this is a theoretical number because some of this fat could go to muscles. But it just shows that even though it was just an extra 50 calories, they add up over time. The key is, a lot of our choices are very small but because of repetition and longevity, the results can be disastrous.

Chapter 3 – Are blacks cursed?

"The Negro is an unfortunate man. He has been given a black skin. But that is as nothing compared with that greater handicap that he is not permitted to receive the Priesthood and the ordinances of the temple, necessary to prepare men and women to enter into and enjoy a fullness of glory in the celestial kingdom [i.e., godhood]."
~ *Apostle George F. Richards, Conference Report, April 1939*

Simple answer to the question: It is all in our minds. It is called MINDSET.

We all know the bias against black people, including racism. We have heard about instances where dark skinned people have been subjected to unfair treatment. I read a news article recently where a young man called D'Arreion Toles in St. Louis, Missouri, USA was stopped from entering his apartment just because he was black. Part of the article from the news reads as follows:

> *D'Arreion Toles said he was coming home from work when neighbour, Hilary Brooke Thornton, physically blocked him from entering the luxury block in the Missouri city.*

Mr Toles posted a three-part video on his Facebook page, which has now gone viral, showing the woman standing in the doorway of the building demanding he show her his key and tell her his unit number.

Alongside his posted videos, he wrote: "Woman tries to stop me from coming into my building because she feels insecure, Downtown St. Louis luxury loft, because she doesn't feel that I belong, never really thought this would happen to me, but it did!

"I was shocked this is America in 2018!"

Ms Thornton was fired from her job as a luxury realtor after the video provoked outrage.

The above is just to highlight that, yes, it is true that blacks are usually subjected to unfair, racial treatment, especially in developed nations where they are the minority. It happens and I wanted to make that clear.

Having said that, are we, the dark-skinned, cursed? I don't believe that to be the case. We are not cursed. I am black and have some challenges in life just like anyone alive, but the colour of my skin played no role in that. No black person is cursed. That argument is just a silly stereotype.

Unfortunately, some of us the black folks use it as an excuse. Are we disadvantaged in some instances because of the colour of our skin? Absolutely. Is that the case in Africa? Absolutely not. We are in charge. We are the majority, unlike in America or Europe or Australia where blacks are the minority. So, my fellow African, our destiny is in our hands.

We cannot and should not even imagine that we are cursed. Trust me on this one. I know what I am talking about.

The trouble is not people of other races looking at us and thinking, "oh, black, what a cursed colour", but Africans or blacks in general looking at their skin colour and thinking, "I am too dark and I must do something about this." I have seen and heard black people making statements like, *I am black but not as black as that guy,* referring to another black person. Because of this attitude towards our own skin colour, there is a new industry that is booming – the skin-lightening industry or bleaching.

According to The Guardian, this industry was worth around $4.8 billion in 2017 and projected to hit $8.9 billion in 2027. To be fair this is global value, not just African. Having said that, statistics indicate that a high percentage of African women use skin-lightening creams compared to women of other races. I was reading an article by Ronald Hall,

Professor of Social Work, Michigan State University, where he was talking about what he calls "The Bleaching Syndrome." The article states that in countries like Togo and Nigeria, over 50% of women use some form of bleaching products to make their skins look lighter. This is all due to the stigmatisation associated with being too dark skinned or black. That is dumb, if you asked for opinion on this. Being lighter doesn't make you better let alone smarter.

But a lot of people from my black race are having none of it, and they believe the darker colour is impacting their marriages, careers, and all the good stuff. Please refer to the following excerpt from article from a study conducted by the University of Cape Town about this very topic of skin bleaching (by M. Davids, Lester & van Wyk, Jennifer & Khumalo, Nonhlanhla & G. Jablonski, Nina. (2016). The phenomenon of skin lightening: Is it right to be light?):

"Chemicals capable of lightening the skin – variously known as skin-bleaching, skin-lightening, depigmenting, skin-evening and skin-brightening agents – are among the most commonly used skin preparations in the world. Globally, Africa reportedly exhibits a high prevalence of skin lightener use.

The prevalence of skin lightener use across the African continent has become a common part of life in African communities. In the late 1960s, 60% of urban African women reported using skin lightener formulations, making these formulations the fourth most commonly used household product (after soap, tea and tinned milk) ...

The motivation driving the practice is often the desire to lighten one's skin because of a perceived notion of increased privileges, higher social standing, better employment and increased marital prospects associated with lighter skin. This perception, coupled with influential marketing strategies from transnational cosmetic houses using iconic celebrities, increases the allure for women primarily, but also increasingly, men."

All this trouble in the name of lighter or white skin. If we don't value our skin colour, who is? I remember when we grew up we used to have two popular hair products; one was called INECTO Super Black and the other was called Go Black. These products are still sold in some African countries, but they are no longer that popular (you can search for these online). These products are used to dye the hair pitch black; shiny black and we loved them. A lot of people, Africans, valued their blackness. Now instead of improving on that we cherish other cultures (Western) over ours. We have low self-esteem when we are with other races with white or lighter skins. That is very unfortunate.

* * *

We know that people from the Western world usually refer to something bad by referencing dark or a black colour. I have been in situations where a white person would use black to define a bad situation. It doesn't usually feel good even though the person making the comment is just saying that with no reference to a black person whatsoever. Sometimes the realisation by the white dude that there is a black guy in the room usually makes them feel uncomfortable after using black to refer to a bad thing. They feel guilty or even embarrassed for saying something like that in the presence of a black person.

Some of the common expressions used are:

- Blackspot
- **Black market**
- Black sheep

- **He's got a black heart**

- A dark period in our history

- The future looks black

Below is what the English dictionary says about black as used to explain something bad:

"If you describe a situation as black, you are emphasizing that it is very bad indeed."

Why is our colour used as a definition of bad? Is it associated with Africa, because that is where you can find the most extreme cases of bad stuff done by black people? And that the blacks are usually associated with negative, bad stuff? Poverty, crime, and all that? Whatever your opinion on this one, it does not matter, and it should not matter. If anything, we could use this negativity as a motivation to prove the "logic or reasoning" wrong by achieving unprecedented success. I am sure you've heard the saying, "the best revenge is massive success!"

Remember that it is all in the mind and whatever we believe as Africans translates to our actions. We must remember that black is just another colour and there are instances where it is used to define good. Like a company is said to be in the black if it is performing well financially. Why not focus on that type of black if we have to choose? It is because we have it all imprinted in our minds. That is the power of mindset.

All I know is that we are not cursed. It is all a load bull for anyone, especially blacks, to think that our dark skin signifies bad fortunes or a curse. Look on the bright side: we don't have to worry too much about sunburns; in fact, we don't have to worry about that at all. We have natural tan.

The problem is that a lot of Africans believe that they are cursed. You would hear an elderly person say something like, *we the black people are cursed* based on the sufferings we see in Africa. We compose songs to show or tell the story of our plight and in most cases the songs are about asking God to explain why we are in such a dire situation, that is, what did the Africans do to deserve so much punishment. We never sing about taking ownership. There is a Zulu song from Maponya's Egoli play and below are some of the lines from the song (Theatre and Change in South Africa, Contemporary Theatre Studies, by Geoffrey V. Davis and Anne Fuchs):

Tixo Somandla: God Almighty

Sibuza kuwe, Senzeni na? We ask you, what have we done?

Sicela kuwe, Somandla: We ask from you Almighty

Suza izitha: Chase away our enemies

Siza iSizwe, Esimnyama: Help the black nation

You can see that this is a song that shows that we are finding fault elsewhere and want the Almighty Himself to provide some answers. Don't get me wrong here, prayer is a good thing and a lot of us get comfort from that, but how about pray or sing to ask for guidance? That is, accept that we have messed up in life due to our poor planning (LIFE CHOICES) and that now more than ever we need the Almighty's guidance to get through this.

This negativity is something that I believe gets implanted in our brains from a very young age and then we grow up with that sense of resentment towards the successful people. Instead of learning from them, we sing songs to blame them. Not only that, we sometimes feel inferior when we are with white people.

Have you ever seen a white man walking amongst black Africans in the heart of an African shopping centre? The level of confidence he shows, regardless how low his IQ may be, would amaze you. You see a man with unmatched levels of confidence and self-belief. He may be a complete moron for all we know but, that is beside the point. He walks like a person who owns everything around him. That is because he was raised to believe in himself. And if he were to go to the village, he would be treated like God. He was raised outside the negativity of song.

I recall when I did my induction training for a mining company in Australia and one of the topics covered was around racism and discrimination, and the Aboriginal people were covered on that lesson. One of the things that the instructor mentioned was that the blacks in Australia (Aboriginals) tend to be shy and reserved with a low self-esteem. She went on to say compared to New Zealand native Māori, who are dark or black in colour, the Aboriginals have lower self-confidence even though both nations have whites as the majority. This is because the Māori never allowed themselves to be subjects of the settlers. They stood their ground and it paid off. I remember thinking to myself at the time, *hmm, aboriginal people are just like Africans. We tend to value white people more than we value ourselves.* Even the Jesus Christ images that people hang on their walls are of a white man, even though scholars believe Jesus was dark skinned. A lot of Africans are brainwashed to believe that Jesus was white.

I know that it is a belief in other cultures and religions in Africa that if you have a dream at night that involves a white person, the elders and *prophets* will tell you that it signifies that God had visited you. This is crazy of course but it is still happening in our continent. It is a psychological thing and when we go to sleep and the subconscious mind takes over, we start "thinking" or dreaming about those things we associate with whites. And when a white dude appears in our dreams we think God had paid us a visit. What a load of rubbish! Unbelievable nonsense to be honest.

* * *

Botswana, for instance, is a country that still has capital punishment. Some years back there was a love triangle crime that involved a mistress, the late Mariette Sonjaleen Bosch from South Africa, murdering the wife of her boyfriend. This is based on the facts of case or the court's verdict. They were all whites from Polokwane, South Africa. Mariette Sonjaleen Bosch was sentenced to death and was eventually hanged. This became the biggest news ever in the history of Botswana at the time. The main discussion was down to the fact that a black government had sentenced and executed a white person. I am sure there were other blacks that met the same fate at about the same time, but their executions did not create so much murmuring. Death penalty is bad as far as I am concerned. The saddest thing for me was that the focus was around the executed person's skin colour and it felt as though the government wanted to show who was the boss, which was a pity. Instead of talking about the sadness of losing another human being, we talked about the first white woman killed in Botswana by the black government. We spoke about it as if it was okay for the white governments to kill black people.

It is an issue of value. We put a very low price on our heads. The same applies even in cases where we know for a fact that we are treated unfairly. A colleague of mine, who is married to a white woman told me a story about a time when his car bookings at a car rental in South Africa were messed up. Basically, they kept the wrong car for him, even though on email they had previously indicated that they would have the right car he had booked. Just a day before he travelled to Johannesburg, South Africa, he got an email indicating that they, the car rental people, had made a mistake and that they had given his car to someone else by mistake. *We apologise, and blah blah,* they said as they would normally say even though we know that they don't mean it and don't care. They do it all the time anyway, why would they feel sorry this one time?

Anyway, he says he did not respond to that email because he was furious. The other reason was that he believed he would easily lose the argument anyway so why bother. As he was seething and wondering the best cause of action should be when he got to South Africa, his memory bank came to his rescue and he unleashed a *better plan*. When they landed in South Africa, he explained the situation to his wife and he also explained the stereotype and bias about the South African system. He told his wife that for them to get the car that was 'rightfully' theirs she would have to get her ass to the counter and do the talking. He didn't say it like that of course. It turned out to be a master stroke because the next thing he saw was his wife holding the keys for a brand-new Mercedes Benz car. Not only did they get a new car, but they got an upgrade at a discounted price *"for the trouble we caused you ma'am,"* they said to her.

Who knows, maybe if my friend had gone to the counter to plead his case he would have gotten the Mercedes Benz too, we will never know. But he says he was not willing to take his chance given the history of blacks and whites in South Africa.

I could relate well to my colleague when he explained this and I too believe that he would have lost the battle. The bigger picture here is that blacks probably allowed this rubbish to happen for so long that it is easy for white South Africans to just abuse us like that. Don't get me wrong here. I am not saying blacks just allowed the whites to abuse them in South Africa. But I am just saying that even after apartheid ended we still have doubts about how whites view us. We must value ourselves higher. We tend to believe that we would lose a case even when both parties know that we are totally right. Like I said, these are seeds planted in us from childhood. What bothers me is that sometimes we don't even realise that we are relinquishing our power and control to the other person; the white person. We do all these subconsciously without noticing that we are "screwing" ourselves.

A lot of African countries still don't get it. We subconsciously believe that whites or people from European and Asian countries are better than us. We just don't realise it at times I guess. In Botswana we had a mining company called BCL Limited where almost all the leadership positions were held by whites from South Africa. Starting from as low as what was called a Mine Captain, it was all whites in white overalls and white hardhats (white helmets). And it was considered "appropriate and as expected" for something like that even with locals who were more qualified and smarter than the white dudes.

It is true that other races (continents) are ahead in terms of the developments but that doesn't make them smarter than us. We just happen to not like to keep up with the rest of the world in terms of developments and following a better path I guess. If we are as smart, why not keep up? Low self-esteem and lack of belief in our abilities.

Think Differently

If we don't value ourselves, nobody is going to. Value is perception and if we perceive our value to be less than that of other races, then rest assured that those other races are not going to place a higher value on us. Have you ever gone to a supermarket, saw a product you like priced at $15.00 for instance, looked at it and went, *nah, I think they made a mistake, this is worth $22.00 and that's what I am going to pay for this item?* I think we can both agree that that is unlikely. In fact, knowing how human beings reason, we would probably think you are on drugs or something like that and that maybe you need to be committed to a facility. That is because normal people don't usually place a higher value on something than what the owner does. Yes, we may think to ourselves that something is undersold but to say it out loud to the salesperson is unheard of.

If we, the Africans or the black race, undervalue our skin colour and by extension our race, don't expect anything better from others.

What I am saying here is that we must change our way of thinking. These is not rocket science because regardless of how we look at it, based on the situation we are faced with in Africa, it shows that our thinking is probably (excuse my language but frankly) crap. It must stop. We must change. This whole nonsense of placing a higher value on others than ourselves is a demented way of thinking. It means we are "slaves" to our belief system. We consider other races superior to our race and for that we subconsciously expect the other races (white in most cases) to do everything for us and we remain consumers. Why can't we make mobile phones, cars, televisions, and all that? The information is out there in the public domain if we need it. The problem is that we lack the will, the desire, the belief that we can do it.

For me this is the main problem. I have seen this even in the workplace where a certain individual is considered the smartest and they are the ones who settle arguments or disagreements. Now, if you are in that situation, you are literally making yourself a *slave* to the *smart* guy. The *smart* person does most of your thinking and whatever they say stands and that is our problem. The fact that most us, the African people, tend to blame our misfortunes on the colour of our skin is a huge problem.

We must address this crazy stereotype. That is very important. We must place higher values on ourselves and not only stop there, but also challenge ourselves to prove that to ourselves. It is common knowledge that we, as human beings regardless of race, usually perform only up to the level that we believe we are capable of. If you believe that you are capable of just making a toy car, that's all you will achieve. You are unlikely to think about making a real car because you have defined your capability and put a limit on what you can achieve. Africans must believe that they can achieve anything they want to achieve.

Our attitudes must change and that is one the most important areas that should be addressed.

Some of the *little* things we can start with include the following:

- Most of us know the proverb, *charity begins at home.* As parents we must instil in our children the belief that the colour of their skin shall never play any role in their lives;

- We must value ourselves more and this include even the colour of our skin. Forget about being lighter because that only shows people that you are insecure;

- Have self-belief and higher self-esteem. I used to sit at the back at school many years ago because I did not believe I was good enough to sit in the front rows. I would sit and slide down on my chair to avoid being seen (more like hiding at the back). I could never raise my hand to answer a question in class. My self-esteem was terrible but later in my life I realised that that was damaging. That is something we can teach and train our children on and encourage them to make mistakes and even give small presentations at home to improve their confidence;

- Believe in our capabilities and that we can achieve great things in life. We must neither be slaves to our thoughts nor to the past. Colonialization happened a long time ago. It is in the past and we must focus on the future. Brian Tracy once said, *successful people tend to face the sun so that the shadow stays behind.*

Chapter 3 Summary

- Blacks don't value the colour of their skins and some believe that the dark colour is a curse;

- African women are the main consumers (per 100 users) for the bleaching products, in an effort to make the skin colours lighter;

- Our self-esteem needs some working on;

- Remember that your value or self-worth can never be more than what you place on yourself;

- Train our kids to believe in themselves.

CHAPTER 4 – The Blame Epidemic

"Blame doesn't empower you. It keeps you stuck in a place you don't want to be because you don't want to make the temporary, but painful decision, to be responsible for the outcome of your own life's happiness."
~ Shannon L. Alder

"If you could kick the person in the pants responsible for most of your trouble, you wouldn't sit for a month."
~ Theodore Roosevelt

How is it possible that two adults can have contrasting interpretations of the same event playing out in front on them? I was reading an interesting book recently that I believe answered this question very well. The author defined this as *Mental Filters.* He explained that the reason we end up with two grown-ups coming to two completely different interpretations of the same event is due to what he calls mental filters. He defined mental filters simply as what we learn as we grow up; how we were raised, the type of education we got, the people we associated with, the political climate we grew up in and so forth. Basically, the way we interpret an event is all down to our history and life experiences. Based on those past experiences, we tend to almost always come to different conclusions about the same event.

This is the reason we view things differently in Africa. In fact, this is a universal thing. But back to Africa, we have people who look around and all they see are Europeans, like in Zimbabwe, who came into their country and destroyed their livelihood. Still in Zimbabwe, you have people who look at the Europeans and wonder, *what can I learn from these people because they have some skills that I don't have?* When that happens, people call you all sort of names including a puppet because in their eyes these people are evil.

Africans must acknowledge that there is a serious problem when most countries or the rest of the world is moving forward while we seem to be engaged in a reverse gear. Our general growth trend is very slow.

We are living in an era of information technology where all the information we need is as far as the palms of our hands. We have smartphones and access to the Internet, but we don't want to use these phones to improve our situation. When we are asked to explain our not so favourable situation (as in why our lives are so tough), most of us blame it on the West. It is like we have a serious *blame epidemic* or a *blame pandemic* disease. It is a pandemic because we don't want to move on and we hold grudges forever. We tend to blame racism for most of our problems. We are convinced that the reason we are where we are today boils down to what the colonisers or settlers did to us. A lot of us feel like it was the settlers that must shoulder the blame for most of Africa's troubles. It is true that the settlers entered our continent by boat, stole our land, and did all those terrible stuff to our great-grandparents. Africans are entitled to feel aggrieved. The problem is we don't want to move on with our lives. We enjoy living today in the past.

Before you accuse me of taking sides and defending the settlers, let me reiterate that I feel sorry for my ancestors for what they went through. It was a living hell for most of them. They were kicked out of their fertile lands and forced to work for settlers at meagre pay rates, and that is if they were lucky to ever get paid at all. A lot of them worked for nothing. These were terrible acts and we cannot and must never forget them. That is as far as we should go. What I mean is that we should have these acts recorded in our history books for the future generation to know what their ancestors went through; the sacrifices they made, the abuses they suffered. Just history and leave it at that. No grudges. No revenge. No blame because there is nothing to gain but everything to lose.

Believe me when I tell you that there is no pain worse than blaming someone for your problems while they just keep getting better and better. It is like trying to get someone's attention only for the other person to ignore you. You feel insulted. You are seeking attention, but no one gives a toss because they have more important things to worry about.

Blaming others for your problems can be a brutal feeling. I have lived it in my past life and I know how bad it can be. You become psychologically and mentally drained and blind to your failures. It is a disease that can be cured. I suffered this disease early in my career. I complained all the time; at work, at home, at church, everywhere.

I used to believe that some people were intentionally working against me to ensure that I failed at work. I felt insecure and forever looking over my shoulder. If I entered a room and found people having an innocent laugh, I would conclude that they were making fun of me. Over time, I started associating with the negative-minded bunch where our discussions were around people who *always wanted to be seen with senior management.* We failed to realise that in life you have to associate with the right people to succeed because that is where you learn about success. We called them *ass-lickers* because they wanted to progress by selling their souls to management. Our belief was that the reason we were not moving forward was because of what they were talking to management about and that it was about us. As these go-getters went about their business, progressing their careers we started suffering severe *blame* syndrome. Instead of learning from all these high performers we just despised them, complained and blamed them for our failures. It is a bad feeling I can promise you that.

Let me reiterate this point again and that is our history is not a pleasant one when it comes to colonisers and being racially abused in our land. In fairness there is a lot of truth in our cries. There was a lot of suffering, but not in all the African countries I must add. Botswana for instance, never went through some of the brutal experiences that the likes of South Africa went through. South Africans suffered. We know about what the late Nelson Mandela and his *partners-in-crime* went through. It can be painful to see someone enjoying the benefits of your land while you suffer and that brings me to the next topic.

South African Apartheid

"Yes, I learned history at school; I know everything about apartheid. My dad, he bought the books about it, stuff like that. But I just move on with my life. It's completely different for me."
~ Caster Semenya

"Like slavery and apartheid, poverty is not natural. It is man-made and it can be overcome and eradicated by the actions of human beings. Overcoming poverty is not a gesture of charity. It is an act of justice... Sometimes it falls upon a generation to be great. You can be that great generation. Let your greatness blossom."
~ Nelson Mandela

This beautiful country called South Africa, is an African economic powerhouse. There are a lot of contentious issues in South Africa but the most divisive one is land expropriation without compensation. If recent events (as of January 2019) are any indication and based on the news we read, South Africans are facing one hell of a challenge. I feel sorry for President Cyril Ramaphosa. He has an overflowing plate and if he can get over this issue unscathed then we would know that there is a strong leader down south. I hope that they emerge on the other side of this a much better nation.

South Africa used to be to Africa what USA is to the rest of the world. That is slowly changing though. And I think one the main reasons for this slow decline is that there are lots of people who still blame the settlers for their current problems. And I will remind you again that there is nothing wrong highlighting your concerns and past injustices. Just don't get stuck on them.

By the way I can pick any country in Africa, especially Sub-Sahara Africa, and talk extensively about their challenges too. The reason I am choosing South Africa is that it is a very well-known country in Africa with a lot of history, most of which is recent like apartheid *(Translated from the Afrikaans meaning 'apartness')*, and many other well documented stories and land expropriation without compensation comes to mind. The other reason I chose South Africa is that when you watch the news or interviews done with the poor South Africans who live in shanty towns the one thing that keeps popping up is apartheid. That is, most if not all their troubles are down to apartheid.

Please note for the record: Apartheid was a terrible, evil policy that neither I nor any African I know condoned and I am thrilled that it ended. Having said this though, I must say that some of the things I am going to say in the next few paragraphs may be offensive to others and I apologise in advance.

This book is not about apartheid and forgive me if this topic takes too much of your reading time. I am using apartheid to define the underlying problem regarding our culture in Africa. Again, I am in no way pretending that I know a lot about what went on down south other than what I read and was taught at school. But just hear me out and pass judgement later. You are entitled to your opinion, and we all are. The next few paragraphs are just my opinions. Now that we have this taken care of and it is out of the way, let's talk about apartheid, just a brief history, shall we?

The apartheid policy – *or shall we call it the demented ideology* – was officially introduced as law in 1948 by the minority white led government of the National Party (NP) in South Africa (*or Suid-Afrika as it was officially called by the racist regime*).

But it is worth noting that the system existed well before 1948, the year when National Party got into power. There were segregation laws that were passed prior to 1948 and it was only after 1948 that apartheid was made law. The

National Party just legalized it and the white minority started to *legally* use the state's apparatus like the police and the military to brutalize the majority black South Africans, coloureds and Indians – *legally* because it was the law of the land as far as they were concerned. Obviously, it is never legal to brutalise another human being. How evil can you be? This was beyond bad. To legalise evil is truly unbelievable. But they unashamedly did those suckers!

The system was designed to ensure that whites enjoyed an unfair advantage over everyone and most did not feel guilty about that because as I said, it was legal. It was taught in schools and at homes and the white children grew up knowing that they were entitled to the riches that South Africa offered.

These guys were mean and brutal based on what we have read. They were ruthless and the police ensured that the law of the land – apartheid – was upheld. This situation made it almost impossible for blacks to make any headway in terms of their lives. They became beggars in their land. Personally, I think the most devastating law was the Group Areas Act:

> **Group Areas Act, 1950** – *This was the act that started physical separation between races, especially in urban*

areas. The act also called for the removal of some groups of people into areas set aside for their racial group.

Promotion of Bantu Self-Government Act, 1959 This Act said that different racial groups had to live in different areas. Only a small percentage of South Africa was left for black people (who comprised the vast majority) to form their 'homelands'. This Act also got rid of 'black spots' inside white areas, by moving all black people out of the city. Well known removals were those in District 6, Sophiatown and Lady Selborne. These black people were then placed in townships outside of the town. They could not own property here, only rent it, as the land could only be white owned. This Act caused much hardship and resentment. People lost their homes, were moved off land they had owned for many years and were moved to undeveloped areas far away from their place of work.

Some other important laws were the:

Prohibition of Mixed Marriages Act, 1949

Immorality Amendment Act, 1950

Separate Representation of Voters Act, 1951

(Source: https://www.sahistory.org.za/article/history-apartheid-south-africa)

These are good reasons (not excuses) for black South Africans to complain about their hardship. There is no denying that. But let me remind you that it is 2019 as I write this book and apartheid ended back in the early 1990s, well over 24 years ago. A lot of people are arguing that it would take upwards of a century even for the scourge of apartheid to disappear.

It will take time, no question about that. Having said that, I believe there should be genuine indicators to show that the lives of black South African are improving. A clearly defined plan of action by the government and the citizens, for that matter, to get themselves out of that scourge. Maybe with Cyril Ramphosa as President that might change because he recently unveiled the African Nation Congress manifesto that is aimed at improving people's lives. I hope he succeeds. There has been some progress I must admit, but it is too slow and not keeping up with the nation's challenges.

They have a corrupt government, just like most African countries. South Africa was recently led by none other than the man from KwaZulu Natal, Msholozi, Jacob Zuma, a very corrupt man (again based on well documented facts). You must have heard about Nkandla homestead? Those rondavel huts and kraals and chickens? It cost the South African taxpayers a whopping R246 million plus. This was a controversial topic that dominated the news for some time and it eventually led to Zuma's downfall. It is sometimes referred to as the Nkandlagate.

The Zuma administration had nothing planned as far as addressing the ills of apartheid. The very people who voted them into power continued to suffer under his rule. Their motto was simple – loot the country like the whites did and make sure that the whites suffer the same fate as the blacks did. Revenge was the name of the game. Who benefits? Not many and the majority suffer. The late Mahatma Gandhi once said an eye for an eye will only make the whole world blind.

The two evils that dominated the era of Zuma were revenge and blame. It was a perfect combination for failure. Corrupt leadership that blamed apartheid when Cape Town was running out of water.

Only a fool can claim that apartheid wounds can heal overnight. Of course not. Everyone was touched by apartheid. People lost their lives, those who survived lost their loved ones, others lost their land, others were imprisoned (Nelson Mandela is a good example).

I was reading an article (www.news24.com) where the author wrote the following:

> *"Did you know that fewer than 2,000 people were killed by security forces in South Africa during the 42 years of Apartheid? And did you know that 80% of all the politically motivated deaths during Apartheid (total 20,000) was due to black-on-black (mostly tribal) violence?"*

To be fair, the journalist did say that he didn't imply that 2,000 deaths were okay. He was challenging the fact that people speak of the apartheid evil as if it was the worst thing ever while on the other hand Robert Mugabe was killing thousands of his people in Zimbabwe. I think he forgot one important fact and that is this black-on-black violence was a tool used by settlers to ensure that blacks fought each other – the divide and rule philosophy.

I have dwelled a lot on this but as I mentioned before, I could have easily picked Botswana, where we have our own problems. I will touch a bit on some later.

Anyway, I have laid bare my case against apartheid. It was horrible and even shocking that racism still exits.

You may ask, so what is your point here? Good question.

Our actions are determined by what we believe. Someone once said, *it is all in our minds.* That is, the more the black South Africans (including the government) believe that there is nothing they can do and that they are doomed for a long time and blaming it all on apartheid, then the more likely it would be for my fellow Africans to remain poor. Our thoughts define our emotions and the actions we take and choices we make tend to reflect that. For our South African friends, those feelings of hopelessness would shape their actions for as long as they live unless they view life from a different perspective.

Apartheid has ended. It ended at least 24 years ago. Yes, not a generation ago, but still a long time. The point I am trying to make here is that, yes it will take time of course. But what we must all see is a process. A process that shows that the country is heading in the right direction as far as the people's lives are concerned. That the corrupt are jailed.

Most people born in 1994 are working today and some are married. Are we arguing that it takes way more than a baby to be born, raised, graduate from university before we can start seeing progress? I don't think so.

The apartheid chapter is history, a painful past that we all wish it never happened, but it did. Unfortunately, we cannot change that. And that is the case with all past events. They cannot be changed but we the poor people love to *fantasize* about things we can't change. Before we start complaining about our past and the circumstances we find ourselves in, how about we start thinking about the future? Oprah Winfrey once said: "Step out of the history that is holding you back. Step into the new story you are willing to create." Simply put, forget about the past because you cannot change it and focus on the future.

Note what Caster Semenya said, she said "yes, I learned history at school; I know everything about apartheid. My dad bought the books about it, stuff like that. But I just move on with my life. It's completely different for me." She is South African and most of us know some of the challenges that she goes through on a day to day basis including what the International Association of Athletics Federations are making her go through. But she says *get over it and move on.* Casper Semenya is my inspiration.

I remember listening to Mr. Vusi Thembekwayo, a wealthy South African entrepreneur and motivational speaker, when he said he would sponsor a Kenyan over a South African to start a business any day (you can watch him on YouTube to realise the importance of this). What struck me the most about what he said was that the worst thing to happen to South Africa following the end of apartheid was the Black Economic Empowerment (BEE) initiative.

(Just FYI: BEE is a government initiative aimed at addressing some of the challenges that blacks, coloureds, and Indians faced during the apartheid era. They can now access financial help from the banks, own shares in companies and so forth. In fairness, it is a well-intentioned initiative but poorly managed and implemented. That's my opinion anyway.)

Mr. Thembekwayo's argument is very simple to understand. What he is saying is that you basically get someone who has no clue whatsoever about running a business, let alone entrepreneurship, allocate them over 20% of shares in a company they have no idea how it was started nor the sacrifices the owners made to be where they are, and expect them to run the business well. He says what he saw were people getting a free ride to a company and having access to over 20% of the company's share, which is millions of dollars in some instances, and the next thing you see is a person driving a Range Rover. The problem with BEE is that people feel like they are entitled to free stuff. I will talk about entitlement later.

Why are so many South Africans still talking about apartheid? Why are Zimbabweans (Mugabe and his cronies) still obsessed about the British? Why are South Sudanese still blaming their Arab counterparts in Sudan for all their troubles? It is the same story for many countries across Africa. We must change.

To summarize this apartheid discussion, all I am saying is that, yes, it is hard in South Africa just like in many other African countries, but we have to leave the shadows of the past behind and move forward. You cannot forget the evils of apartheid. But, you can use that painful past as a fuel, like a rocket fuel, to propel yourself to greater heights.

Change – Can we leave the past behind?

The secret of change is to focus all of your energy, not on fighting the old, but on building the new. Life is not about wasting your energy fighting!
~ Socrates

Are we capable of turning it around? Absolutely; no question about it. But have we got the will? That is probably the most import question to ask. Do we have the at-all-cost will, the burning desire, to change? To accept the past and stop blaming others and work our way to prosperity? I am sure we can do it.

It is said that you should worry about the past only when you want to use it for the *lessons learned*, not to beat yourself to death with club about what could have been, hence the saying, *forget the mistake, remember the lesson.* The past should be used as a guide or a reference. We can change the course for our future. Africa's time is now.

It is our time to change. If we don't change, it is going to be the same for generations to come. For Africa as a continent to change – by change I mean ending poverty, see developments and fortunes that most of us desire – her people must change and stop blaming others. We must be different people. Thomas Jefferson, the 3rd USA President once said, "If you want something you've never had, you must be willing to do something you've never done." I am sure you have heard the saying *insanity is doing the same thing over and over again and expecting different results*.

It doesn't take a rocket scientist to see that we have serious problems in Africa. Just visit any village in any African country and you will realise that there is something that we aren't doing right. Unless we are happy living in shanty towns of course, which I doubt. In rural Africa you will find it all; abject poverty and very little hope for the future. When these wonderful people wake up, most follow the same dead-end routine:

- Wake up in the morning, wonder what is for breakfast and eventually realise that there is nothing;

- Pass the morning gossiping about others – usually those who are well off – and accusing them for corruption and ritual killings;

- At around lunch time, they ask themselves where their meal was going to come from. Again, no answer. Alternatively, do what we refer to as *eating with your feet.* This is where you strategize and decide which family to visit at lunch time so that they can serve you. It is coordinated where you make sure that you don't visit the same family every day;

- With lunch out of the way, they continue with the talking, which again has nothing to do with ideas to turn their lives around. To be fair our people don't really know much other than poverty (I am not saying it is okay though);

- Dinner is considered a luxury. Nobody thinks about it. If anything, that time is used to plan for tomorrow's meals, i.e., where to go to get a plate of food;

- Twenty-four hours later, the cycle is repeated.

- That is how most of the African citizens in rural villages spend their days – worrying about basic stuff. There are people doing well in Africa, don't get me wrong, but they are a tiny minority.

When I say *we can change the course of our future* I am making a general statement, which is true for any situation. It could be apartheid, war, life of crime, anything. Someone might say, *well you weren't there,* or *you are not South African, what do you know about apartheid?* Yes, that would be true because I am not South African, I didn't live through the horrors of apartheid, but principles are universal. We have seen people rise and succeed against tough odds. South Africans and all African countries can too.

The biggest problem is this:

We are too fixated on the past and losing sight of the fact that the land of milk and honey is in the future.

It all feels like people want revenge, especially when you listen to some leaders. This is what we must root out. I just wanted to use apartheid as an example for everyone to realise that there are big issues that need our undivided attention. And these are African problems. Blacks' problems. It has nothing to do with racism. It is the truth and until we remove that racism veil covering our faces and accept that these challenges are ours to address, then it will be the same for many generations to come.

I guarantee you that many people are going to ridicule me for stating this. Too many of our people are angry about the injustices of the past and rightfully so. But we must be mindful that if we are not careful that anger will take over and control our thinking. Why not channel that anger into something positive? Give a motivational speech. Write a book. Start a charitable organization.

There are thousands or even millions of Africans who are doing very well under tough conditions. They are not happy about their past either, but they chose to follow a different path. You don't see them sitting under tree shades all day drinking local beer discussing *why it can't be done.* That it is so difficult and there was nothing they can do. They do not accept that they are condemned to a lifetime of suffering and poverty.

Let us start this change. It starts with you. Myself. My friend. A family member. Let us not get bogged into some silly stuff like witchcraft. My families used to fight all the time accusing each other of witchcraft. It was full on and we, the younger generation, joined the fight by default just because our ancestors fought, so we had to continue the fight. There was so much hate amongst ourselves. All we knew was that there was witchcraft involved and our families were *killing* each other through the dark magic of witchcraft. We had no proof of who killed who; the *prophets* told us the lies as they usually do and we believed in their wicked prophecies. How silly! But we believed and fought. I am happy to say over time some of us saw the light. The situation is much better.

This tale may not come close to the pain that we live through every day in Africa. Things like hunger, corruption, crime, drought, vote rigging or electoral fraud, HIV/AIDS and other diseases, poor sanitation, apartheid of course and many other ills. These are the challenges that have ravaged Africa for way too long and far too many people know only these as the only reality. A lot of people were born and died in these conditions. It is all they ever knew. But it would be silly for us to give up and accept this as a normal and that we cannot change it.

You probably are asking yourself, "but what can we do?" Well, there are no easy solutions. The first step is to change ourselves. That is the first and most important step. I am not a wealthy man, but my life is fine. All I did was change my view of life. My hatred of past events controlled my future actions and I was living a miserable life. Changing your views and looking at the future with optimism is all it takes. Your actions will change. You would start thinking about saving even as little as $50 per month and still be happy.

How about you *step out of the history that is holding you back. Step into the new story you are willing to create* as Oprah says? This is only possible if we rid ourselves of the *blame epidemic* disease. Tell yourself that you or Africans cannot continue like that. Draw a red line and say, "this is it, I have had it" with this life of mediocracy and stupidity, because it is. Stop blaming others.

If you go into social media during periods like Black Friday, you will see the type of vitriol that is being directed at the Americans. The belief is that Black Friday originated from those years of slavery where the slave owners sold slaves at a reduced price. I saw the following comment on the social media about Black Friday:

> *"The term 'Black Friday' originated with the practice of selling off slaves on the day after Thanksgiving. Now do we really need to embrace this kind of torture? Or we are so foolish, that we don't even research what is this so-called Black Friday..."*

I don't know and maybe that was the case, but frankly, we must move on. I am not saying FORGET. All I am saying is that we cannot be defined by the bad stuff that happened many years ago. How about we research about what we need to do to improve our fortunes rather than about some stupid day where people get stuff for half a price? Remember I said you don't have to forget. Holding grudges isn't going to help you though.

* * *

You don't have to change the world for your life to change. I came across this tale somewhere online and apparently it was told some time in 1100 AD and goes like this:

"When I was a young man, I wanted to change the world. I found it was difficult to change the world, so I tried to change my nation.

When I found I couldn't change the nation, I began to focus on my town. I couldn't change the town and as an older man, I tried to change my family.

Now, as an old man, I realize the only thing I can change is myself, and suddenly I realize that if long ago I had changed myself, I could have made an impact on my family. My family and I could have made an impact on our town. Their impact could have changed the nation and I could indeed have changed the world."

Change yourself first and you will be surprised at how contagious that is to the rest of your family. I mean that in a positive way. Your positive attitude will rub off the rest of your family and all those that you associate with. That is what we must do in Africa. Change ourselves and blame no one. The past is important of course, but it is gone, and we can be smart and define our future based on lessons learned from the past mistakes. The good thing is that it doesn't have to be your mistakes that you learn from. You can learn from other people's mistakes, which should be easy given that Africa has lots of them.

Start with yourself. You can start a positive vibe that spreads like wild fire – a positive inferno. Have a positive outlook about the future.

It is our thoughts about the past that are holding us hostage. That is an obstacle we must rid ourselves of. Hal Elrod defines this as a Rear-view mirror syndrome, which he eloquently expressed as follows:

> *"We go through our lives, our subconscious minds equipped with a rear-view mirror, through which we continuously relive and recreate our past. We mistakenly believe that who we were is who we are, thus limiting our true potential in the present, based on the limitations of our past."*

Taking Responsibility

"The price of greatness is responsibility."
~ Winston Churchill

"When you think everything is someone else's fault, you will suffer a lot. When you realize that everything springs only from yourself, you will learn both peace and joy."
~ Dalai Lama

You will only feel better when you own up to your actions. It is called taking responsibility. When you accept your mistake or a failure then you are considered a mature person. If you believe that the only way out of your predicament is to point a finger at someone else, then you are still an infant; maturity is doesn't exist in your vocabulary.

Is it easy to make it in Africa? Absolutely not. If you live in Africa, say South Sudan, chances are that someone living in USA, for instance, would probably be hundred times better off in life for the same effort they put in that a South Sudanese puts in for the same period. Just think about getting ice in your beer. How easy do you think that would be for a South Sudanese young man living in village? Probably close to impossible. That is the reality that we live in. It is hard just to find clean drinking water in South Sudan. By the way, the Americans or anyone for that matter, do not have to apologise for that. They earned that privilege, and it doesn't matter how. I just want you to note that this scenario is not meant to solicit sympathy for Africans. I am just stating the fact and answering the question I asked at the start of this paragraph.

It is tough in Africa. The living conditions in some parts of Africa are inhumane. But who is going change that? You are right; the Africans. Forget about the Messiah coming to rescue us one day. It is never going to happen. We are in a deep hole. How did we end up in that hole, you may wonder? That my friend, is a moot point. How we get ourselves out of the hole is what matters. We have to take responsibility.

The challenge is having the majority of Africans accept that this is a problem that we have to get ourselves out of. People with this type of a mindset are in the minority. The majority of us believe that it was apartheid. It was colonial rules. Or that the Americans or Europeans are still stealing our resources. We even blame God for the drought, that His Almighty is not providing us with enough rain to be able to farm and feed ourselves. But there are places in Africa that have fertile soils and enough rain like the Democratic Republic of Congo (DRC). According to https://www.export.gov/ the DRC exported about US$77m worth of agricultural products in 2017 and it imported US$109m worth of agricultural products. Almost double. DRC has more fertile land than it needs to sustain itself let alone export to other countries. But what are they doing with it? Nothing is the word I am looking for. Zimbabwe used to be referred as *Africa's breadbasket* when the Europeans were doing the farming. Instead of learning from them, we saw occupiers (yes, they were) and decided to kick them out without any concrete plan. What a waste.

We have to take responsibility. That is the first step that needs to be taken. If I were to refer to the topic of apartheid in South Africa, the country has massive potential. Even though the whites did some deplorable acts on the black majority, they still set proper infrastructure that would have allowed the new government to improve on. But the new guys had one thing in mind. To loot the country and punish the whites. That is being irresponsible. To improve our situation in Africa we must take the responsibility and act. We should not hope that someone is going to feel pity and get us out of the hole we are in.

> *"You can't hire other people to do your push-ups for you!"*
> *Jim Rohn*

I cannot imagine a better metaphor for responsibility. For you to build muscle or lose weight you must put in the hours yourself. There is no way around it no matter how much money you have. That is responsibility. Accountability.

Why is responsibility such an important factor in our lives? I think it is the first step that a person must take to address their challenges. Deciding to act independently.

We must ignore that rear-view mirror and look to the future with optimism and determination. This is a rallying cry.

Attitude

"Attitude is a little thing that makes a big difference."
~ Winston Churchill

My view and attitude towards life changed a few years ago when I was listening to the late Mr. Jim Rohn, one of the top philosophers of all time I believe, saying that when he joined the ranks of adulthood after quitting college he was a serial complainer, grumbler, whinner, and all that negativity you can imagine. He complained about everything, from the corrupt government to the greedy private companies all the way to the rich who think about themselves only. This kind of grabbed my attention – a whinner – because the more he spoke and the examples he gave, the more I felt like I was listening to real-life story about myself.

Years before hearing Jim speak, people closest to me used to tell me that I needed to tone down my negativity. They were basically shouting *when are you ever going to take responsibility about anything?* I did not want to believe them and felt they were jealous of me, but subconsciously a tiny bit of my inner self knew that these people were right. I could not and would not accept that. I couldn't because I just told myself that I was a *smart* Engineer from a reputable university. It is human, it is African. We hate it when people give us an honest and constructive criticism.

Anyway, as Mr. Jim Rohn spoke I got interested and listened on. He said he complained about:

- His low pay (which he later, in hindsight, realised that it was just reward for what he offered considering his value or lack thereof to the company he was working for at the time);

- That tax was too high (which did not help given how corrupt the government was as far as he was concerned);

- The prices for daily essentials were too high, that everything was overpriced by the big corporations who were out to swindle him and people like him of their hard-earned cash. That the poor working class were targeted by these companies. He resented big companies and successful people.

He said he just didn't want to accept that he was living a life of mediocrity.

But he says that his perspective on life changed forever after he met his mentor, the late Mr. Earl Shoaff. He says after narrating his problems to Mr. Shoaff, the response he got changed his life forever. It was a total and complete paradigm shift. Mr. Shoaff gave him a pep talk about life and explained to him that it was true that he needed more money to address all his challenges but that he disagreed with him on one thing, and that was, the root cause for his problems. Yes, he needed more money to deal with his needs as we all do. *"The problem is that you do not have ideas on how to generate money Mr. Rohn, that is your main problem. All it takes is just one idea to turn your life around,"* Mr. Shoaff told him.

This got me thinking too and I thought *wow, this is gold!* By the way we all go through moments like this where it usually takes something like listening to a talk or reading a book or a motivational quote and you get that chin-holding-moment and go "hmm."

Before you worry about the lack of funds, have you got an idea that you strongly believe can be a viable business? We usually get our priorities wrong and worry about money or the lack of rather than worry about how to make money – an idea. We want to have the money before we even know what we are going to do with it. That is the wrong attitude my fellow Africans. The right approach and hence a good attitude, is to have an idea first and then think about the money.

This talk that Mr. Jim Rohn gave was my rebirth. I just decided to cast away all the negative energy I possessed and start looking at life differently. A change of attitude. That's all it takes. Again, I am not saying changing your attitude of negativity is going to solve all your problems. But I can guarantee you that a negative attitude will make them worse. In my case, that change in attitude cost me a few relationships, very close relationships for that matter. My attitude towards life was completely different. I took ownership of my actions. I became a responsible person. You too can stop blaming others or the past. You can leave the past behind. It is not easy. It takes some serious commitment.

Attitude and responsibility are partners-in-crime. Changing your attitude means you are more likely to own up to your actions, which is being responsible. We cannot move forward if our attitude towards white South Africans apartheid changes. If we are forever blaming the colonisers for our problem (wrong attitude), our future wouldn't get better.

We have a whole range of reasons (by "reasons" I mean a polite way of saying excuses basically) to explain our mediocre lifestyles. Africa is probably the harshest place on planet earth to grow up. To be frank I cannot imagine a more punishing environment to be raised than ours. It is a tough place to grow. The African child goes through a lot from birth to adulthood. But who is going to save us Africa? Maybe we are waiting for Our Lord in Heaven to send the Messiah, His one and only Son who died on the Cross, to come and save us. I am sorry to be the bearer of the bad news because that is just pure fantasy. It is never going to happen. We are going to have to save ourselves and show the world that we are trying before we can get help. In fact, The Quran's *Ar-Ra'd* 13:11 says, *Indeed Allah will not change the conditions of a population until they change what is in themselves*. It doesn't matter what your religion is, the important thing is the message. Let us get rid of the thought that the West is going to improve our lives. All these donations are doing nothing but making us beggars. We all know the expression that says,

> *"Give a man a fish and you feed him for a day; teach a man to fish and you feed him for a lifetime"*

All these handouts we are receiving from the West are just an international welfare program that is condemning us to recipients of handouts. Remember that Mr. Donald Trump is never going to send us the best and the cream of the United States of America. Did I hear, *"of course, what do you expect? The man is racist."* If he is, I love him for it because it can only mean one thing, and that is, force us to think and work hard for ourselves rather than expect the Americans or the Chinese to bail us out. That is the attitude we must instil ourselves and our children. The attitude that we can do it ourselves.

By the way, I am not saying *thanks but no thanks* to gestures from the developed nations. We do appreciate their help. My main concern is that we are becoming too reliant on outside help. I sometimes can't help it but imagine that maybe with the history of apartheid and slavery we tend to think, subconsciously, that the mess we are in was caused by the white people and therefore they must help us. It is their fault therefore, it is their responsibility to fix the mess. I believe we have that going on in our minds at a subconscious level. Yes, they did some terrible stuff to the black people, but I don't believe that it is their fault that we are still in this terrible situation. We must change our attitude and take the responsibility to get ourselves out of this.

Our way out of this mess

The following points outline, briefly what we can do to address issues outlined in this chapter. In the simplest way possible, all we have to do is just change our view of life.

- The world doesn't owe us anything. For us to move forward we must stop blaming the past. Former Australian prime minister Mr Kevin Rudd once apologised for the treatment that the Aboriginal people received from the whites, which is commendable. But what did it achieve? Did their lives change following that? You can check online. If Africans want the Americans to apologise for slavery and Afrikaners to apologise for apartheid, well they can demand it and probably get it (of course not from America with Trump as president) but that is not going to change anything. We are the ones who can change it. At this moment there are too many of us standing on the path of change. Brian Tracy once said the problem with the poor people is that they never forget. We hold grudges for life. So, I say to you my fellow brothers and sisters, stop blaming others. Look at yourself, your past and look at people around you who are doing well and see if there are lessons you can learn;

- I said we have everything in the palms of our hands and I meant getting that smartphone and putting it to good use. Read about Patrice Motsepe. Read about Strive Masiyiwa. How about Ali Mufuruki? These are men who made it in Africa;

- Take responsibility and own up to the problems we are faced with. We may get apologies and all that but, that is not going to change our fortunes. Responsibility is realising that it doesn't help you to sit under a tree and talk about others and accuse them for your suffering. It is realising that you graduated from university and that if you can't find a job, sit under that cool tree shade, write ideas of business opportunities, and I am sure one of those ideas will lead to something. This ties in with the bullet point above. You have to read to have an idea of where to start;

- Attitude – until we change our views about life and developing positive attitude, it is going to be almost impossible to move on. If we believe the whites are not giving us the respect, maybe it is time for us to earn that respect. We continue making the same mistakes every year and expect other nations to respect us. When some of these nations accuse us, we play the race card. That my friend is some attitude – a bad attitude!

Chapter 4 Summary

- "If you could kick the person in the pants responsible for most of your trouble, you wouldn't sit for a month." – Theodore Roosevelt. No need to elaborate on this one;

- If we continue blaming others for our problems we will never make any progress in our lives;

- We must take responsibility, individually and collectively, and get ourselves out of the mess we find ourselves in;

- Be accountable. If we keep referring to the past for our current problems, we will have enough reasons to continue living mediocre lives, and we will have enough excuses to do nothing;

- The world owes us nothing and we must get used to it.

CHAPTER 5 – Conformance

"He who joyfully marches in rank and file has already earned my contempt. He has been given a large brain by mistake, since for him the spinal cord would suffice."
~ Albert Einstein

"Do not follow where the path may lead. Go, instead, where there is no path and leave a trail."
~ Ralph Waldo Emerson

"Great spirits have always found violent opposition from mediocrities. The latter cannot understand it when a man does not thoughtlessly submit to hereditary."
~ Albert Einstein

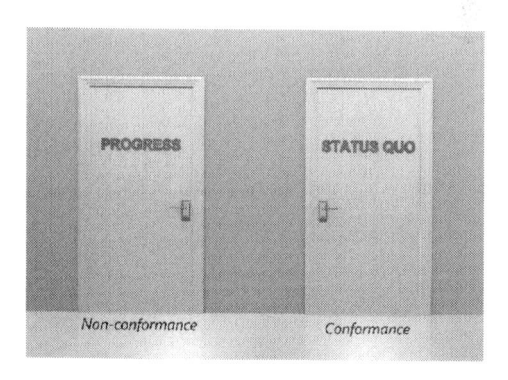

You've probably heard the expression, *"you become an average of the people you associate with."* If your friends or people you spend time with are successful, then by the law of averages chances are that you will be successful, or at least try to succeed in life. That is because successful people spend most of their time talking about financial independence and other topics aimed at improving their lives and for you to fit in you are going to have to *toe the line*, otherwise you would be the odd one in the group. It is called conformance. We conform to the environment that we spend the most time in.

I was reading an <u>article</u> online about this very topic (conformance) and this is what the author of that article wrote:

> *To learn what is correct, we look at what other people are doing. In his bestselling book, Influence: The Psychology of Persuasion, psychologist Robert Cialdini writes, "Whether the question is what to do with an empty popcorn box in a movie theatre, how fast to drive on a certain stretch of highway, or how to eat the chicken at a dinner party, the actions of those around us will be important in defining the answer." Social proof is a shortcut to decide how to act.*

That explains the reason you see:

- men peering on fences in Africa;
- so many empty cans or litter all over the place;
- more taxi cabs than customers at Gaborone taxi rank;
- so many street vendors selling the same products or fruits at one common location.

It is mainly because of conformance. We do what others around us do regardless of whether it is right or wrong. That is how we fit-in in a society.

There are pros and cons for conformity. Like in the example I just gave about associating with the right people and working hard to be successful and being financially independent. I believe that is a good form of conformance. The downside to conformance is that sometimes we tend to blindly follow the crowd (the so-called herd mentality) without thinking about the consequences. The response you get is "because everyone is doing it."

In the previous chapter I wrote about blaming others instead of taking the responsibility. That is mainly because most of us are born and bred in that environment. We become part of the problem without realising it. Other times we are more concerned about how people would react if we behaved in a *different way.* A situation where a person knows that there is a problem, but they don't have the guts to challenge the status quo. We tend follow the same dead-end-path that everyone is following with the knowledge that it leads nowhere.

Since the majority of African kids grow up under these types of environment, they consequently conform to the norm. It is the law of averages. We spend too much time talking nonsense and playing victim, and our children learn this behaviour too, and their children do, and on and on. It is a vicious circle. For us to exit that circle requires what scientists call an exit velocity. It is that velocity that once attained, you gain enough force to propel you out of this vicious cycle. That exit velocity can be likened to knowledge and education as discussed in the first chapter. Because once attained, that's it, you are gone and never coming back.

We don't have any other choice but to change. Let us challenge ourselves and commit that we cannot continue like that. I am not implying that if we change course today then we are all going to be rich and wealthy the next day. All I am saying is that we commit to start a new journey. A journey is a process. You are not always going to complete the journey you start. It is impossible to achieve everything that you set out to achieve. But you have try and not give up before you even start for fear of what others would say. I can assure you that if you were to start that process, that journey that many are avoiding (because of the shackles of conformance), those who come after you (your children, relatives, loved ones or friends) will take over the reign and continue. At least they wouldn't be starting from zero. That is how we must break free from bad conformance.

The failure to make any measurable progress is because we conform to mediocrity. Most Africans seem to be content with what they have, which is very little and sadly this is a situation that is moving from generation to generation. Our children grow up in an environment where there is little hope.

The good news is that there are successful people in Africa that we can look up to for motivation. The likes of Patrice Motsepe of South Africa. Or Zimbabwean businessman Strive Masiyiwa. These are people that all Africans must aspire to emulate – the strong, the believers, goal-setters, ambitious, the go-getters. The club of winners. Why did these guys and many others like them achieve success? They stood out in the crowd. They are like zebras in the middle of donkeys (not in a mean way because we normally associate donkeys with laziness).

Not only can you learn from these successful individuals, but from others' mistakes too. Those that we can look at and say, "I never want to be like that!" There are too many of this kind. Robert Mugabe of Zimbabwe. Joseph Kabila of the DRC. Jacob Zuma of South Africa. Tedodoro Obiang Nguema Mbasogo of Equatorial New Guinea, who unashamedly appointed his son as his vice president (I still can't get my head around this one). Omar Al-Bashir of Sudan. Jose Eduardo Dos Santos of Angola. King Mswati III of Swaziland. Mind you this list is for presidents and kings; the well-known people. There are many others that fly under the radar and I am sure you have seen some in your area. They are poisonous and just doing the opposite of what they do is probably all that you need to start your journey to success.

Pettiness

"You don't have to knock anyone off their game to win yours. It doesn't build you up to tear others down."
~ Mandy Hale

"Those who occupy their minds with small matters, generally become incapable of greatness."

~ *Francois de La Rochefoucauld*

Recently I read a news article where a famous USA hip hop rapper 50 Cent bought 200 front-row seats tickets to a concert by another rapper called Ja Rule so that the seats stayed empty throughout the concert. The two guys have been in a feud since the 1990s and keeping the seats empty was meant to be a constant reminder to Ja Rule throughout the concert. You may think, *who gives a toss, it is just those stupid, spoilt rappers fighting for nothing,* but I wonder why is it that this type of rubbish is common with black artists? It is called pettiness and we know that neither 50 Cent nor Ja Rule wins this battle.

I do not want to paint all blacks with the same brush. There are lots of decent men and women in Africa and the world over. Having said that, I think sometimes we can be extremely petty and hold grudges for generations. Forgive and continue is something that is not very dear to our hearts. Mind you, we are not born petty – we just happen to conform to what we see happening around us. It is a habit that we learn as we grow up. There is a lot of anger in most of us and we channel it towards things that are not helping us.

How can we stop this madness?

This is probably one of the hardest to change because conformance is what society expect of each one of us. One has to be bold and say *this is not working for me and I cannot continue like this.* Jim Rohn called this "the day that turns your life around." It is about taking a stand. If you are in a group of people and the topic of discussion is about some dude who thinks he is smart and likes doing things differently, then maybe that is the guy you need to catch up with.

- Remember that you are your own person. The influence from others can be too large to ignore but before you follow the crowd, ask yourself whether what you are just about to do is the right thing or not. We have to change course because whatever it is we are doing at the moment is not working for us. Whatever we are stuck to and conforming to is not serving us well;

- Stop being petty and be supportive of each other. Napoleon Hill once said, it is literally true that you can succeed best and quickest by helping others to succeed.

Chapter 5 Summary

- "Conformity is the jailer of freedom and the enemy of growth," John F. Kennedy;

- We conform to mediocrity and sometimes we are even ashamed to do the right thing because we wonder what people would think about us;

- You can learn from the bad. Just look around you and you will see thousands of people doing crazy things. All you have to do is commit to doing the opposite;

- Too much jealousy in us leading to pettiness that is holding us back.

CHAPTER 6 – Of Breadwinners and Entitlement

"If a man will not work, he shall not eat."
~ New Testament, 2 Thessalonians 3:10

"There was a time when only men could provide or work, and still a lot of countries are like that. But there's a price to be paid for that when you're expected to be the full-time caretaker and you're expected to be the full-time breadwinner."
~ Patricia Arquette

"The rise of families from the ground doesn't depend on the son or daughter who studied medicine or law. It depends on every family member who is tired and fed up with living conditions as a family. The guts to try gives you the chance to prosper. But of most importance is being able to organise your family and work as a team on the road to building family wealth is a remarkable move. Surprise yourself, give yourself time and undertake that idea you have. Now go and make money legally."
~ Kemo Mabina (a young ambitious Motswana)

I cannot think of a race that embraces this breadwinner phenomenon more than African people. We have families, sometimes in upwards of ten in one household, all looking up to the eldest child in the family and expecting them to support everyone. It is a culture where people feel entitled to be supported and looked after by the poor breadwinner of the family.

The bible says *if a man will not work, he shall not eat.* Unfortunately, this does not hold true in Africa providing there is a breadwinner in the family. My fellow brothers and sisters, get moving. Do something. Anything. It doesn't matter as long as it is legal, just do something.

Sipho Mbele, a South African author once posted the following on his Facebook timeline (this is an edited version because there were some Zulu phrases used in the original post):

> *Taxi operators walk away with R200 a day and that's R5,600 per month.*
>
> *A waitress earns R2,500 to R3,500 per month*
>
> *The street vendor that sells fruits and sweets at the corner. They bank R4,000 come month end.*

And you're sitting at home earning R0.00 pm and won't be a taxi driver or a waiter because you're educated, yet you're an expense at home. Ushota ngama Cosmetics (you need cosmetics), *data, airtime, etc...*

Guys we need to face the reality and take whatever comes our way. Times are very hard. R5,600 per month is a lot of money.

"BAZOTHINI ABANTU" syndrome (what will people say syndrome) *does not pay your bills or put food on the table*

All you like to do is share jokes on Facebook and window shopping all day at the malls, you don't want to hustle.

I really feel sorry for the 65-year-old parents that still need to go to work for their kids while they are taking selfies all day and posting on Facebook.

Vuka (Wake up) & Start Doing Something... anything.

You may agree or disagree with his numbers, but the message is simple. Do something. Too many young, able-bodied men and women don't want to do anything. In some instances, they are picky on the types of jobs they are willing to do. I am talking about someone without a job but still having the luxury to decide which job they can or cannot do. A man in his 30s living with his parents, with no job but telling you that he cannot do labouring jobs like farm work. How can you possibly explain and defend that? The thing is, "why worry when I know that the breadwinner has got me covered?"

This is a very serious disease where breadwinner sons and daughters are almost held prisoners by their families. Every pay check from your employer is supposed to be shared with your family. As soon as money start rolling in, your siblings quit. They just throw in a towel, stop whatever it was they were doing and go home to stay with their parents usually at the village. The breadwinner is now made a modern-day slave serving his or her family – parents, siblings, nieces, and all. Every month end one of the siblings jumps on the bus and heads to town where the breadwinner is working; to get the *allowance* for the following month's expenses. The poor breadwinner even pays for the sibling's bus fares for the round trip.

Africans like to receive at all costs. We like the free stuff. It is so ingrained in our hearts and souls to an extent that we don't even notice it. I remember when I went to the United States for my studies, I became a *pen collector* because there were so many everywhere I went. In USA and many developed nations for that matter, when you go into an office or a bank you would normally find a lot of pens in a small cup so that people can use them for their paperwork. The idea is that you fill up your forms and when you are done you put the pen back in that cup. Very simple, right? Not for me. All I saw was an opportunity to take free stuff home. When I look at my kids, the contrast is stark.

This may sound like it is nothing and you may even say *who cares, it was just a pen and what has it got to do with anything?* True, it was just a pen and the act wouldn't have led to, say prosecution for instance. But that is not point. The behaviour is the problem. That is the underlying issue. The culture of wanting to receive stuff without breaking sweat. Accumulating wealth without action just like the recipients from the breadwinner.

It is perfectly fine for a child to support his or her parents. In fact, it is said that blessed is the hand that gives than the one that receives. It is a great feeling when you are in a position to help your parents. Embrace it, cherish it, don't feel guilty about it. But it is wrong for people to assume that since their brother or sister or aunty is working then they don't have to worry about doing something for their lives. To throw in a towel and quit as soon as we realise that there is a breadwinner in the family is wrong. We stay home with our parents and say *we will eat what our parents eat.* How can this be okay?

The Age of Entitlement

"You cannot help people permanently by doing for them, what they could and should do for themselves."
~ Abraham Lincoln

"If this country is ever demoralized, it will come from trying to live without work."
~ Abraham Lincoln

"You have to do your own growing no matter how tall your grandfather was."
~ Abraham Lincoln

Let me give you a true story about the former president of Botswana, Dr Seretse Khama Ian Khama aka SKIK, to explain this behaviour entitlement. *(Disclosure –I was not his biggest supporter when he was president, but I will try and give you the facts about him, and you can decide for yourself whether it is a typical example of entitlement or not.)*

Seretse Khama Ian Khama is one guy who believes that whatever he wants, he must get. As at the time of writing this book (Jan 2019) he was in a power struggle with the president of the day, Dr Mokgweetsi Masisi. Yes, you heard me right, power struggle even though he is an ex-president. The problem is that he wants to rule from the grave, as some people call it. This is how it is with our former president, SKIK:

- His father, Sir Seretse Khama, was the first president of Botswana;

- SKIK appointed as a Brigadier General (Deputy Commander) of the Botswana Defence Force (BDF) at only 24 years by his father, who was the president of Botswana. For me this is corruption but his supporters don't want to hear any of this;

- He went on to become the Commander of the BDF in 1989 when he was 36 years old. Note that the guy only held two positions in the Botswana military – the last two top ranks on the BDF – Brigadier General and Lieutenant General;

- He went on to become the vice president of Botswana from 1998 to 2008;

- Then he became president of the republic in 2008 until his retirement in 2018.

Show me a person who thinks this is normal and that it happens all the time and I will show you a liar. You can see that SKIK had it easy all his life. SKIK never followed the normal progression path that the rest of the soldiers at the BDF have to go through.

With regards to the power struggle, it turns out that when he retired as president he made a deal with the then vice president, Mokgweetsi Masisi, to appoint his brother Tshekedi Khama as the vice president of Botswana when he (Masisi) became president. SKIK acknowledged this agreement. Long story short, Masisi rescinded on that apparent agreement and appointed someone else. In Masisi's defence, I think it would have looked corrupt for him to appoint Tshekedi as the vice president. This did not go well with Seretse Khama Ian Khama as you can imagine because what he considered *normal* was being turned upside down. For him *normal* is where he gets whatever he wants. This is a classic example of a person living a life of entitlement.

Personally, I don't think that is the worst part of this unfortunate story. The worst part is having so many citizens defending SKIK. Okay, there may be other agreements that we are not aware of or that there are other things that Masisi is doing to the poor guy, SKIK, we don't know. At the moment it is Masisi's words against Khama's. I don't care about that fight. My concern is that some of our my fellow countrymen and women choose to ignore the simple fact that SKIK wants to have it all and had it easy all his life. Why should it be okay for the presidency of the country to move from father to sons? It is not a monarchy. People say Donald Trump is a narcist but at least he worked hard for most of what he has. SKIK did not earn most of the riches he has. Again, I am not his biggest fan and this is probably a biased example. But entitlement does that to you. You believe that you must get whatever you want. The guy even wants to continue flying the BDF planes. Come on... that must not be defended.

* * *

I don't mind paying taxes and I know that a lot of people share this view, for as long as the money is spent wisely. I just have negative views about welfare, where some people feel that it is alright for them to stay home, do nothing and receive free cash every fortnight or monthly. There are people who need our help, don't get me wrong. The Bible says, "it is more blessed to give than to receive" and the

Quran says, "... it is better for you to spend in charity." Forgive me if I am being religious. Helping others in need is fine. For someone to feel like they are entitled to get welfare is wrong.

You will recall the story at the beginning of this book about the riot we had at our high school because we did not like the free food? Or the Black Economic Empowerment in South Africa where blacks are given a free ride into owning businesses with limited skills on running businesses? It is the same with siblings throwing in a towel when faced with life challenges, going home to live with their parents because big brother or sister is working. These are the hallmarks of people who feel like they are entitled to free stuff. The problem with people who feel entitled is that they don't care about others. The fact that other people have to pay higher and higher taxes to support them while they do nothing is the least of their concerns.

When we rioted, we were on free education, staying at a boarding school for free, free food, free entertainment on weekends, but that was not enough. We believed that we were entitled to better food. For me the food we had at the time at school was an upgrade of what I had at home. So, what gave us the right to fight and riot for better food?

Better from what? We were just being spoilt students. We did not care whether the poor were getting help or not. And we grow up to be adults who want the government to do everything for us.

John F Kennedy, the former President of the United States once said:

> "Ask not what your country can do for you – ask what you can do for your country."

Do you share the same view? If you do, excellent. In Botswana, I feel like the culture of entitlement is probably worse than anywhere else in Africa and this is not an exaggeration. This could be down to some of the programmes and initiatives that the government of the day usually introduces in the name of poverty alleviation. These so-called poverty alleviation schemes are usually introduced to entice people especially towards the elections. I will give a couple or so that I believe can be potentially good but the problem is the intention. Like I said some are introduced to get people's votes:

- One that involves having people with small farms to plough and plant crops on a 5-hectar area (500m by 100m) and the government pays you for doing that.

All free of charge! There is no accountability. All that you have to present is a ploughed field with planter tracks of the ground to show that you planted, whether there are crops or not is immaterial. By the way, people get free seeds too. I think it is poorly managed with too many loopholes. Maybe it is a well-intentioned initiative, but the problem is that people just plough and plant, run to the agriculture department, register to have the area taped, then just wait to receive a check. You don't even have to go back to the field after the agriculture officer has measured;

- There is one where you register with agriculture department and the government buys you 11 goats – 10 females and 1 male – and give them to you for free. It is a first-come-first-serve scheme. No skills required on how to look after animals. But what happens is that people get these free goats and sell them to the butcheries. Again, no accountability;

These two initiatives can address some of the struggles that our people face on a daily basis if they were well managed. Sadly, nobody cares. What people care about is getting these freebies. The other problem is that when the opposition parties raise these concerns and asking for people to be held accountable when given these free stuff, the public don't like it. We all know why that is the case. They want to continue receiving these things for free.

I touched a bit on Black Economic Empowerment earlier. It is another scheme that is probably well-intentioned, but the problem is that it is just one of those where you get something that you did not work hard for. You get partnership in a major corporation just because you were disadvantaged by a white minority government, therefore the government is trying to correct the wrongs of the past. The problem is, it is just another welfare scheme.

Albert Einstein once said that "sometimes one pays most for the things one gets for nothing." In our case in Africa, the cost is that we end up with a society that wants to get everything for free. That is a heavy price. The governments are now expected to finance all these welfare programmes with nothing in return.

Men-children and Women-children

"To Raise a child, who is comfortable enough to leave you, means you've done your job. They are not ours to keep, but to teach how to soar on their own," ~ Author unknown

"The greatest gifts you can give your children are the roots of responsibility and the wings of independence,"
~ Denis Waitley

- If Sepas doesn't move out of our parents' home why should I? She is the eldest and I am staying put;

- Meleko is the eldest son and if he doesn't get married then why should I be rushed into getting married?

You may think I am pulling your leg, but these are not jokes or fake stories. They are common discussions taking place under cool tree shades in African villages; real conversations and in some cases, arguments leading to serious infighting between siblings in many households. These are the types of behaviours and attitudes that must be dealt with for Africans and Africa to join the ranks of mature nations. Usually the root of all evil is the issue of inheritance. Adult children staying with their parents with the hope of inheriting whatever they live behind when they die, regardless of how little it is.

This is the case with many families around Sub-Saharan Africa. We just don't like moving out and starting our families. So, Madiba EC remains a man-child, gets married, have children at the parents' and there is nothing wrong with that, as far as we are concerned. This is a huge problem and it must be fixed. By the way, I am referring to myself here. I stayed at my mother's for a long time. Looking back at it, I sometimes wonder *what the hell was wrong with me?* At least I saw the light. You too can. We all can see the light.

The Americans have the expression that says, children must live better lives than their parents. One way to promote that belief is for parents to promote independence. It is unheard off for a 25-year-old man to be living with their parents in the West.

Can we fix this?

It all boils down to education and setting higher expectations. People that are content with just surviving rather than improving their living standard. We lack the necessary education. The education or maturity of understanding that there is more to life than just living with your parents so that you survive through the support of a breadwinner. The maturity to set higher expectations for yourself. We must:

- Encourage our kids to be independent. Moving out of our parents' homes doesn't mean we stop supporting them;

- Your country doesn't owe you anything. Please remember this always. Living with this knowledge will unshackle you from the chains of entitlement and set you on your way to independence;

Chapter 6 Summary

- For as long as we continue with the belief that the one family member working is expected to support every other family member, it is going to be hard to get ahead in life. If you compare an African graduate just starting work to An American, both on the same salary, the American gets ahead much quicker than the African dude or girl who is expected to share their salary with the entire clan;

- We believe more in welfare than going out there to do the work ourselves;

- The idea of man/woman-child must end for us to see progress in Africa.

CHAPTER 7 – Of Ideas, Potential and Fear of Failing

"If you have an apple and I have an apple and we exchange these apples then you and I will still each have one apple. But if you have an idea and I have an idea and we exchange these ideas, then each of us will have two ideas."
~George Bernard Shaw

"What good is an idea if it remains an idea? Try. Experiment. Iterate. Fail. Try again. Change the world."
~ Simon Sinek

"There is no heavier burden than an unfulfilled potential."
~ Charles Schulz

There is no denying that Africa has massive potential to become a global power. The thing with potential is that, if unexploited it will remain just that, a potential. It is the same as an idea; a brilliant idea that is not implemented is useless. It is just as good as no idea. Africa has a lot of potential and by this, I am not referring to abundant natural resources but some brilliant ideas within the minds of millions of our people. Chances are that you, the reader have a few too. Each one of us has at least one idea in them.

Everything starts with an idea. That chair that you are sitting on or a bed that you sleep on or the light bulb that you are using to read this book all started as ideas. But the world would be worse off if these innovators had kept these ideas and died without sharing them. Mr. Les Brown, a famous American motivational speaker once said:

> *"The graveyard is the richest place on earth, because it is here that you will find all the hopes and dreams that were never fulfilled, the books that were never written, the songs that were never sung… all because someone was too afraid to take that first step…"*

Just think about it. We go to our graves with a lot of unrealised ideas. Unfulfilled potential that we spend time every day debating whether to share with others or not.

Brian Tracy, in his book Eat that Frog, puts it this way, "it is amazing how many books never get written, how many degrees never get completed, how many life-changing tasks never get started because people fail to take the first step…" It is all down to procrastination, which I will touch on in a bit.

Ideas are what differentiate humans from other species. Just look around you and see what humans achieved by just coming up with ideas and implementing them. Humans have that much power and we are told that we are not even utilising 10% of our brain power. Incredible, isn't it? It is just unfortunate that in Africa we tend to hold back on those ideas and cower and just conform to mediocrity. Why is that? The environment that we are born into.

Let me repeat what I said earlier, and that is, ideas are worthless if unexploited just like potential or stored energy. Unfortunately, like I said before, it seems like this is more so in Africa than anywhere else in the world. I know this because that is where I was born and raised. I know our culture. I lived this culture. That is the sad reality about our continent. That is why I am writing this book with the hope that children in high school level can read it and hopefully change the course that we are on.

We have millions upon millions of people of high intellect and creative minds but are held back by the fear of failing. The fear of "what would people say?" What a shame. This is real and unfortunately it's ingrained deep into our minds.

Just to give a trivial example, if a teenage girl were to jump on roller skates for the first time we can predict that the probability of her failing is high. That is because the girl is trying this for the first time and hasn't mastered the skills of balancing on roller skates. And there is absolutely nothing wrong with that, it is normal. It is just like a baby trying to walk for the first time. It is fine and acceptable. The problem is that in Botswana for instance, that is not *acceptable*. As soon as the poor girl falls, the majority of those in her vicinity would most likely laugh at her. If the same situation were to be happen in England for instance, the reaction would be different. She would be encouraged to try again. In fact, a lot of people wouldn't even react providing the girl isn't hurt. The expectation is that she would dust herself off and get on with it again, over and over until she masters this.

In Zimbabwe, we would laugh at her. Imagine what this does to the girl's confidence? Just that act of being laughed at. It would most likely shatter her confidence. Note that this is just one example and there are millions other situations like this one where people are afraid to try something for fear of being shamed. It could be someone trying to start a business or another person thinking about sharing a life changing idea. But because they were laughed at from young age when they "failed", they are even more scared to be laughed at when they are grownups.

A lot of kids experience this type of negativity as they grow up and the consequence of that is a situation where the majority of African kids and ultimately adults do not believe in their abilities. They know that it is possible to come up with ideas and have them implemented but the concern is, what if it doesn't work out? Am I going to be made to look like an idiot?

I remember at primary school where laughing at others was just the norm. I am talking about being laughed at and made to look like a fool. Being laughed at because you answered the question wrong. In normal settings when a teacher asks a question, a student who knows or thinks they know the answer raises their hand, the teacher would then give the student an opportunity to answer the question. If you don't answer the question correctly, big deal, who cares? But not where I went to school. When a question was asked almost 100% of us would cower and sink lower on our chairs behind other kids because we were just too shy to raise our hands to answer the question. We were afraid because we knew that a wrong answer would lead to being embarrassed. How stupid can a culture be? With no one raising their hands the teacher would normally pick one kid at random, to answer the question. Those were moments you wished you could hide under the desk; the I-wish-the-earth-could-open-and-swallow-me moment.

You are literally made to feel like you are the stupidest kid in class. In some cases, even the teachers did not help because they had a free reign to embarrass and ridicule you in front of all the other kids. We were made to feel unworthy. Before accusing the teachers, you have to appreciate that they grew up in that environment and it was deemed business as usual for a teacher to make fun of you in class. It is only now with the benefit of hindsight that I realise that that was mental abuse.

When I went on to a junior secondary school to do my Form 1 and Form 2 (years 8 to 9 before senior secondary/high school), on our first day at school, during his welcome remarks at the school assembly, the headteacher made it clear that all the lessons would be taught in English except the local language subject (Setswana in my case). In an effort to make it easy for us to grasp what was being taught, we were told that the local language was not allowed. We were all required to speak English. Common sense stuff really because we all know that practice makes you better.

I remember thinking or imagining "how cruel can a person be?" My opinion was that the headteacher was a cruel human being and I wasn't the only one thinking like that. I think it was a great idea from the headteacher. To learn a language quicker, you must speak it. The writing is the easy part because you have the benefit to stop and think before putting it to paper but the ability to link words into a sentence that made sense without pausing was a daunting task. So, practicing it was the best way to deal with that.

Anyway, as the headteacher was making that announcement we started murmuring in disapproval. We were wondering how many versions of broken English were going to be invented. It was kind of funny just having those thoughts. But that was not our main concern. What made us feel a bit restless was the thought of being laughed at. The thing was that even though we were not good as far as speaking English, we could tell if someone did not speak the language correctly, like the wrong use of past or present tenses. We knew that anyone making such an innocent mistake would be laughed at and the expression was along the lines, *"you think you are smart!"* I am sure you can imagine the choices we made. We chose to *break* the school's code of conduct and spoke our native language. No one was prepared to be embarrassed.

You can see the common theme emerging here. It all boils down to the *fear of failing*. The fear of what would people say? How am I going to be viewed after making a mistake? Would I be considered unworthy? These were and are still the difficult questions that most African kids ask themselves.

I am not sure if you have heard about Winston Churchill? He was the Prime Minister of the United Kingdom from 1940 to 1945 and again from 1951 to 1955. He was considered one of the greatest leaders of his time and possibly the best British leader in recorded history. The reason he succeeded was that he believed that success was almost always preceded by failure. He once said, "success consists of going from failure to failure without loss of enthusiasm." He knew that in most cases you have to try, fail, and try again, before you succeed. The late Dr Martin Luther King Jr once said:

> *"Keep moving, for it may well be that the greatest song has not yet been sung, the greatest book has not been written, the highest mountain has not been climbed. This is your challenge! Reach out and grab it... but there is something we can learn from the broken grammar of that mother, that we must keep moving. If you can't fly, run; if you can't*

run, walk; if you can't walk, crawl; but by all means keep moving."

By all means, please keep moving forward because forward is where better things wait. Some of the acts that we were exposed to were considered minor. Like being laughed at when you fell trying to ride a bike for the first time. Just these simple acts of being laughed at are destructive. They suppress the creativity that could be unleashed by an African boy or girl child.

The self-esteem of an African child is generally lower compared to other nations. On average confidence levels are so low that we are always very conscious and judgemental to ourselves as we speak. We critic ourselves as we talk. Because of this we are reluctant to speak up when an opportunity arises fearing what would people think about us. I know it because I lived it. That was how I lived my life for a long time – extremely shy. I am still shy, but now if I say something and make a mistake I don't care at all. I am not ashamed anymore. But before I got to this stage of not giving rat's neck, I was living in fear, literally.

When I was a university student in the United States of America in Missouri I saw firsthand how different we were compared to Americans. They were confident, willing to try answering questions, ready to stand in front of class and give a presentation and if they made a mistake it was okay. Students were encouraged to keep trying. For me it was a different story. First, the thought of attending a lecture was just not fun and if the lecture involved having to give a presentation, then that was unbearable. It felt like standing in front of *monsters ready to savage and eat me*.

That was the image that I managed to conjure and make it feel real. The fear caused by my subconscious mind. My memory bank had all those thoughts from the past where people used to laugh at us when we made mistakes. Mind you, I was a university student and the fear of making a mistake in a foreign country was too much of a burden. But the truth of the matter is that in most case people want you to do well when you are presenting to them. Unless you are in competition of course.

Fear of failing – the killer of dreams!

"Because of self-doubt, the fear of failure, or laziness, most people usually bite off way less than they can chew."
~ Mokokoma Mokhonoana

For decades and even centuries, nations around the globe have faced what some may have considered insurmountable challenges, but through the will to succeed, they still managed to overcome and came out on top. This doesn't mean there weren't failures along the way. People tried and failed, but they didn't stop. They believed and kept trying until they overcame. One famous writer, Dale Carnegie, once said "most of the important things in the world have been accomplished by people who have kept on trying when there seemed to be no hope at all." It is called persistence.

We must admit that as the citizens of this amazing continent of ours, the African continent, we have set the bar so low that we don't even attempt. We give up before we even try. This is how most of us do it and I mean a big majority us:

- We look at a task (or challenge) at hand,

- Plan its execution in our mind while enjoying the breeze of a cool air under a tree shade,

- Come up with as many reasons as possible on why it wouldn't be possible to execute the task,

- Be happy that we have good reasons no to act,

- And just quit.

Just like that! Can you imagine an easier option? You have probably seen a person stand up, stretch the arms high up and started singing, and if so, rest assured that they were singing in celebration of successfully creating a compelling list of reasons to do nothing. We work harder thinking about the excuses of how it can't be done.

Why is it like that for us the black people? First, I think there is an element of laziness. Then we have this big part of us that just doesn't want to fail. We just don't want to fail at all because we worry about the reaction we are going to get from others. Remember being laughed at when you were little at school? Those memories live on.

Procrastination

"My advice is to never do tomorrow what you can do today. Procrastination is the thief of time."
~ Charles Dickens

"It was my fear of failure that first kept me from attempting the master work. Now, I'm beginning what I could have started ten years ago. But I'm happy at least that I didn't wait twenty years."
~ Paulo Coelho

Procrastination is probably a tool used by nature to separate the poor from the successful. I remember a joke by Louis CK when he said the poor know very well how it is like to be wealthy because they are forever imagining it. We the poor Africans know what we must do to live fulfilling lives. We know that there are things we must do on a daily basis to turn our fortunes around to live better lives. I am not even talking living like kings or anything like that. I am talking just living decent lives where we don't have to worry about where our next meal is going to come from or where we are going to sleep at night. It is all mapped very well in our minds. The difficult part is the action.

Our problems stem from procrastination. We spend most of our time fantasising about living wealthy lives. Dreaming is perfectly fine because it usually takes a dream (or an idea) to move to the next level. The challenge with us is that we just can't act on those dreams no matter how positive we feel about them. Most of us know what we must do to change our situation, but we lack the belief to act. We keep postponing what must be done because we worry about the reaction we will get from others if we failed.

The greatest failure is not the one associated with attempting something and getting it wrong. That kind of failure is acceptable because you learn from it. It is the failure not to try that is devastating. Some of you may have heard about the late Thomas Alva Edison. The story says he attempted to make a light bulb a thousand times before he finally got it right. When a reporter asked, "How did it feel to fail 1,000 times?" Edison replied, "I didn't fail 1,000 times. The light bulb was an invention with 1,000 steps."

One contributor on www.quora.com, Debra Sparks Peterson summed it well when she spoke about Edison's "failures", and she said:

> *There is no known number for his failings. Edison may have failed in many of his experiments and in his schooling, but he had something better working in his favour. He had great determination and persistence.*
>
> *He not only worked tirelessly in his pursuits, such as with the light bulb, and had numerous patents in his name, he knew the value of his failures.*
>
> *He was changing technology and shaping the future for everyone. He employed many workers to develop patents in his name, thus guaranteeing achievements and failures.*
>
> *We owe respect to this determined man. His persistence altered our concepts of what mankind can accomplish in spite of the labelling of such an ungifted youth.*

Obviously, this guy was one hell of a persistent dude. Not too many people can keep trying so many times.

But for him maybe he deemed this a case of life and death. That he had no other option but to succeed.

Today we don't have to try something that many times. The reason is that there aren't too many things that haven't been invented. There are over 6 billion people on earth and chances of you trying something that none of the 6 billion inhabitants of earth haven't tried are very small. And that gives us an advantage that the likes of Edison didn't enjoy. We can learn from others' mistakes and thus make fewer mistakes before we succeed.

The problem is that we know about this, but we just don't want to try. Brian Tracy says the average number of times that people try before they give up is less than one. That is because too many of us, especially in Africa, think about what needs to be done, think about it and eventually give up before we even try. That is our problem.

It all goes back to that girl child who fell off the roller skates and being laughed at. The boy that was laughed at and made to feel inferior for answering a question wrong in class. That kid that was laughed at when he or she spoke broken English at school. That young ambitious guy that was told it cannot be done because many others before him have tried and failed, so who does he think he is? Because of this negativity, we end up with a society that is forever delaying what must be done today hoping that tomorrow would be different. This of course, is a habit developed from a very young age and it takes a lot more than "I will do this tomorrow" for something to get done. Things are forever postponed.

Procrastination is born out of fear to fail. Afraid that you are going to do something very stupid and regret it for the rest of your life. A complete fabrication of stuff that is not real.

My wife once bought me a small journal as a present and the cover was labelled "Finish what you've started!" I am still fighting this fight of finishing what I start. It is a terrible habit and hard to get rid of. But I happy that at least I managed to write this book, even though I feel like I could have written it years ago. I am on the right track towards defeating this problem and we all have it within ourselves to defeat procrastination. This is not some form of a motivational speech, I am telling you the fact. It is not easy, I wouldn't lie to you. But it is possible.

Indecision

"Indecision, doubt and fear. The members of this unholy trio are closely related; where one is found, the other two are close at hand."
~ *Napoleon Hill*

I think this is similar to procrastination, except that this one is more like you are left with the act of *pressing the button,* if you will. That last step in the process. But as you are just about to trigger that switch, you hesitate and go into the *"what if"* mode. The thing with indecision is that you want to be 100% correct all the time. You worry too much about the outcome. Procrastination on the other hand is more about delaying; the act of continuously postponing to the future what you should do now.

Indecision is a big part of our lives. It is a devastating problem where we end up with so many lost opportunities because we are too concerned about the outcome. It is acceptable to take a moment to ponder about the potential outcome because it is human. It is part of our thought process and in some instances, it could be a small matter of deciding what to wear to a party. No biggie. But in some instances, that failure to act can be one that leaves a continent with a tag; the Third World.

Turn the corner and note that ...

- Ideas are a good start, in fact they are the best first step you could take, but they are nothing if you don't take the second step. That is, ACTING on those ideas. I had this book idea 8 years ago but until I started writing, it was just an idea that benefited no one. To turn your ideas into something worthwhile, put them to the test and take action and implement;

- Procrastination – it has been proven scientifically that one way to beat this *disease of attitude,* as Jim Rohn calls it, is to start small and work your way up. For instance, don't try to lose 30kgs in a month through exercise if you haven't been exercising because chances are that you will give up within a week. To start small, especially in Africa, means starting with a vegetable garden in the backyard. Just a small plot where you can plant spinach or tomatoes. The problem is that we want to be out of poverty overnight and attempt to own a farm with tractors, sprinklers, labourers and all of what is required to be a commercial farmer with almost zero knowledge of planting tomatoes let alone running a successful business. Let us start small and also understand that it takes time;

- Don't worry about failing because that is the only way you are going to make it. Brian Tracy says there was once a sales organisation that rewarded its employees based on the number of failures they reported in a day. The company encouraged the employees (the sales people) to go out and talk to as many people as they could. During the process they would get rejections and the more rejections they got the higher the reward. The idea was that if they got rejections (or what others would refer to as failures), they would get better at talking to people and ultimately be better salesmen and saleswomen. And that was based on the knowledge that as they got rejected (fail) they got better. The bottom line is, get those ideas into the open, act on them, make mistakes, learn from those mistakes and get better. Do not worry about what other would say;

- If you allow fear in your life, you will never get anything done. With this book, before I started I kept wondering what if people hated this book? It is okay to wonder but it becomes an issue when we want to be perfect the first time we try because it is unlikely. We all want to go out there and do the best we can but chances are that mistakes would be made and that is okay. If you want to be perfect and satisfy everyone, chances are that you will never start. That is where indecision comes into play;

- It is not okay to say, *I thought about it and I have enough reasons to prove that this isn't feasible.* That is what failures do; think an idea through, debate the pros and cons thoroughly in their minds with more emphasis on the cons, execute the idea in their minds and subconsciously make it fail and then conclude that it is a bad idea.

All I am saying here in short is that let us move our continent from Third World to Second World for a start.

CHAPTER 7 – Productivity is king

"Those at the top of the mountain didn't fall there."
~ Unknown

"If a man is called to be a street sweeper, he should sweep streets even as a Michelangelo painted, or Beethoven composed music or Shakespeare wrote poetry. He should sweep streets so well that all the hosts of heaven and earth will pause to say, 'Here lived a great street sweeper who did his job well."
~ Dr. Martin Luther King Jr.

"Folks who never do any more than they get paid for, never get paid for any more than they do"
~ Elbert Hubbard

Consider the following scenario:

> *Two guys are offered jobs for brick moulding; guy B is offered the job at town B and guy C is assigned to do the same job at town C some 100km away. The two guys have the same physicality and are offered $100 per month to mould 100 bricks a day. Too low yes but these are pay rates in most African countries for labouring jobs. Guy B's attitude towards work is "I equate my effort to*

the amount of money I get paid and as such I produce exactly 100 bricks a day."

Guy C on the other hand believes that the tools at his disposal, which are identical to guy B's, have the potential to deliver 150 bricks a day and he goes for it; he moulds 150 bricks every day for the same pay as guy B. That means for every 2 days his efforts deliver what it takes guy B 3 days to produce. Basically, guy C's value is 50% more than guy B.

Given this scenario, it is very likely that the boss would feel bad that guy C is getting the same salary as guy B. She (let's assume the boss is a she) would probably offer guy C a raise. It may not be 50% but it could be a 10% raise, but a raise nevertheless. Over a period of a few years it is likely that guy C would be earning two or even three times more than our friend over at town B, guy B.

Why am I telling you about guys B and C at towns B and C respectively? Well, it is because town B could as well be Botswana in Africa and town C could be China. This is not a joke. That is the reality of our continent. I don't want to say we are lazy, but a lot of us are. All nationalities have outliers; the few lazy ones who want everything for free. On the other hand, African outliers are the successful ones; the few hardworking ones who sacrifice so much in life to earn a living and want nothing to do with life of mediocrity and welfare. These are the people who show high levels of productivity in the workplace. They go to work to do just that – work, not to hold some small group protests complaining about low pay.

Don't get me wrong here. Africans get paid paltry salaries compared to other workers outside Africa and I sympathise. In Botswana, for instance, the minimum hourly rate is P5.79 (roughly $0.55 per hour based on January 2019 exchange rate). That is very low even though one may argue that the cost of living in Botswana is much lower compared to USA for instance. The question is, what can we do to turn this around? There is no quick fix to this, but it is easy. We just have to be a little more productive. In my example above regarding the two guys, B and C, if these guys were in Botswana starting at $0.55 per hour chances are that over time guy C would creep towards the dollar mark per hour driven purely by his productivity.

American major corporations like Apple, Nike, Ford, etc, are setting their business operations in China not just because the Chinese earn way less than the Americans. If that were the only driving force, then Africa would see a lot of these companies opening shop in most African countries because our hourly rates are lower. It is mostly down to productivity. In layman's terms, a Chinese labourer would probably make 10 units of a product whereas someone from Botswana would produce 1 unit of the same product over the same time frame, say one hour. If a Chinese worker gets paid $3.60 per hour and a Motswana gets $0.55 per hour, it means it is cheaper to do business in China because a Chinese would cost $0.36 per unit per hour ($3.60/10 units per hour) versus a Motswana who would cost $0.55 per unit per hour. This is a no brainer especially if we are talking trillions of units. See the graph below to see the productivity differences between China and Africa. We are not even close.

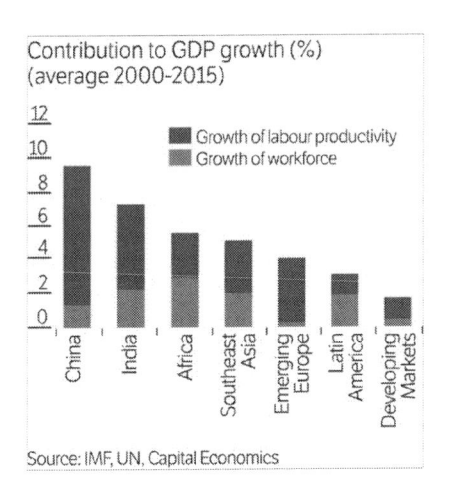

My concern is that most of African workers have it all the wrong way around. Someone would just play around at work and do as little as possible. The general silly argument is that the money being paid doesn't justify doing more. We don't realise that we get paid at the end of a period – like a day, a week, or month – and that means whatever goes into your pocket would be a reflection of what you deliver at the end of that period. Not the other way around. You don't get paid and then do the job afterwards. If that was the case, i.e., getting paid first, then the argument "I am equating effort to money", even though stupid, would probably make sense because then at the end of the month you can legitimately say "you paid me $100, so I delivered to you work equivalent to $100." Whether that is the right attitude or not, it doesn't matter. The point is you would have delivered what you deemed a fair compensation for $100 you got at the start of the period. Even then, I still feel it would still be silly because your employer would never consider giving you a raise with that kind of an attitude.

The bottom line is, one gets paid for the effort put in for the duration in question. Jim Rohn used to say you get paid for the value you bring to the marketplace. If you get paid $100 a month but deliver $140 value, chances are you will get rewarded more with a raise or a bonus just as I explained the situation between guy B and guy C.

I have seen this problem of *I equate the job to the money* way too many times. In Botswana, the government has a programme called **Namola Leuba** (drought relief) where the unemployed do some labouring jobs like picking litter or uprooting unwanted shrubs in their village. It is not work, but a way to help the poor people and the amount paid out is very little and that is not the point because it is not formal employment anyway. The disappointing thing is that these people do nothing but sit under trees all day chatting and laughing. Then at tea break time they get free tea and bread! If you asked one of them why they do so little work, the response is always, "the government is not paying us enough to do what we do!" Mind you, this is not formal employment. People are paid to pick up litter that shouldn't have been there in the first place. To pick litter around their homes. And I am thinking to myself, typical. Welfare. Entitlement. Africa.

When you are offered a job, the employer usually tries to offer you the least hourly rate possible and the reason is that they want to give themselves a leeway to give you more if necessary. That is the reason you can have two employees on the same salary grade or band but earning different salaries at the end of the month even with the same experience. Your aim should be to try and be on the higher end of the salary grade by delivering more.

Most developed countries have what they call Productivity Commissions. These are independent bodies that advice the government of the day about the level of productivity in the workplace across all industries around the country. Not only do they give that feedback, they also tell the government how the country compares to other developed countries. If there is overstaffing in a certain department, they give advice on what the right numbers should be and the government would be expected to make corrections. And it is okay for the government to reduce the numbers. Their focus is to have smaller governments. The idea being that instead of money being wasted on unnecessary resources, it could be used for other worthy causes.

This type of an argument would not be taken kindly in Africa. We believe that it is the role of government to create more and more jobs for people. Government departments are usually wasteful and very unproductive because there is usually no accountability. This is another root of evil in Africa. We have low productivity because "I equate effort to what I get paid at the end of the month," which is very little. The end results of this is that nothing or very little gets done.

Companies around the world know this and that is why most multinational companies are not willing to invest and set shop in Africa. There are many other reasons of course, like corruption, civil unrest, crime but productivity is one of the main reasons. A report from Bloomberg mentioned poor productivity as one of the major challenges facing Africa. Below is an excerpt from the document:

> *For the vast majority of African countries, GDP per capita remains a fraction of the figures in developed and many other developing countries. While a rising population and greater investment should support economic growth, increased wealth depends on faster productivity growth… Low GDP per capita is closely tied to poor productivity in African economies.*

All these problems facing Africa can be overcome because a lot of countries, especially in Asia have faced the same challenges. According to an article (*What's needed to take Africa from Third to First World in 25 years*) written by Sandile Swana and Lumkile Mondi, two lectures of at the University of the Witwatersrand, South Africa, "nineteen out of 23 of the poorest nations in the world are in Africa. Of the

54 African countries, about 19 are represented on the world's poorest list." The article also gives an example about Singapore, under the leadership of <u>Lee Kwan Yew</u>, the first premier of Singapore, as one Asian country that managed to move from the status of Third World to First World in one generation.

Again, *it all boils down* to poor productivity, hence **Productivity is king**.

Complaining all day, all the time

You have probably heard them all:

"The money is not enough"

"It is too hot to work in the open field"

"This is modern-day slavery, and I cannot tolerate it at all"

"Teachers are giving our children too much homework"

"Banks wouldn't loan us their money"

... and on and on, complaint after complaint. It is so contagious that it spreads from generation to generation and it sees no boarders – from Cape to Cairo and east to west of Africa.

Jim Rohn gave a good account of Bible passage about the dangers of complaining in relation to the children of Israel. According to the Bible, the Israelites were freed from slavery in ancient Egypt by Moses and then they had to embark on a long road to the Promised Land, the land of milk and honey, Canaan. The tragedy of the story, as Jim puts it, was that they never made it to this large and prosperous ancient country of Canaan. The problem was that they complained all day, all the time, even though they were free. They started worshiping other things other than God, a big No-No, if you are familiar with God's rule. Anyway, they all perished before they even got to the Promised Land. Because they never stopped complaining.

You don't complain from the word go before doing anything. Things work in the following order and there is no other way:

- You deliver to the best of your ability. Perform to your maximum potential first;

- Then, only then do you get rewarded for your efforts. It is only at this point that you can have some legitimate grounds to raise your concerns if you feel like the reward is not proportional to the work delivered. Be civil and continue performing at the highest level possible (Note that I am not saying **complain** but raise your concerns).

It doesn't work the other way around. Also remember that you don't get rewarded more because you complain more. If anything, you would most likely get penalised for your whinging and complaining.

My boss once rated me "underperforming" for my midyear performance review. Besides the re-birth I experienced after listening to Mr Jim Rohn, this was probably one of the best things that ever happened to me.

Months before this I was on a downward spiral. I complained all the time. It was out of control and that review was the wakeup call that I needed. It was one of those moments where I think a few things lined up very well in my favour. I had just joined a multilevel marketing program, reading self-development books and listening to Jim Rohn's audios as well. When I got a rating of below average, I was really hurt. My initial instinct was that the man hated me. Fortunately, at that stage in my life, I was mentally mature. I remembered what I had been reading and listening to and I started reasoning rationally. First, there was no reason for my boss to hate me. The second thing was that, he was very open, and he mentioned to me that the feedback he got from my colleagues about my attitude was not positive. Then I realised that I had to put what I was reading to good use. It was apparent that complaining had done nothing good for me. I resolved to stop complaining and to knuckle. I worked harder.

The problem is that a lot of us find comfort in complaining. I think most of it boils down to laziness. It is easier to complain than do anything. To this I say, stop complaining and do something. Imagine if Oprah complained about the injustices against blacks in the American system? The world would have been robbed of a great human being. Instead of complaining and taking to the streets, she worked harder. I am not saying you should be an Oprah of Africa. Individuals of that character are rare. I am saying complaining will not take you anywhere. Yes, stand up against injustices but work harder.

One thing I learnt is that people hate it when you complain too much. People have enough problems themselves and they are not ready to waste their time listening to your problems.

Let us do the following to fix our situation...

First, we must agree that there is no quick fix to this problem because like most of our challenges, it took generations for us to end up where we are.

- Productivity – I know that we have some smart and productive individuals all over Africa, but the numbers are a little lower. We don't need a scientific study to prove this. As I mentioned earlier, companies are choosing China over us. Obviously, there are political concerns with Africa but if it were all based on productivity, we would still lose the race for foreign investments. I think the main area we must focus on is training. We should train our workforce to understand the implications of poor productivity. When I attended a mining induction in Australia for a company called Fortescue Metals Group, I couldn't believe how high the standard of training they offered to their new employees was. They would go as deep as explaining the tiniest details about the impact of digger operator taking 10 seconds more than planned when loading a mining truck. Now, a digger or excavator operator at a mine site in Zambia may not appreciate the significance of this *small* detail. And that is the problem that we must address. Training, education that is;

- Of course, we work to earn salaries to look after our families but the advice I got before is that never put money ahead of your performance. Be productive, work as best as you can and everything else will fall into place including money.

Chapter 7 Summary

- You get paid for the value you bring to the marketplace, according to Jim Rohn. That explains the reason why we have people doing similar jobs but getting different salaries;

- It is wrong, in fact theft, to go to work and expect to be paid more than the effort you put it;

- Be productive – when you get to work, work;

- Stop complaining and move your ass.

Chapter 8 – Short Term is Planning to Fail

"Someone's sitting in the shade today because someone planted a tree a long time ago."
~ Warren Buffett

"Give me six hours to chop down a tree and I will spend the first four sharpening the axe."
~ Abraham Lincoln

Successful people, and ultimately countries, think long term. In 2018, Saudi Arabia were talking about Vision 2030. They even had an international conference called **'Davos in the desert'**, A Saudi Arabian initiative aimed at wooing world's top investors to invest in Saudi Arabia; a plan beyond reliance on oil. Just for a moment forget about the political issues with Saudi Arabia and the well-documented record about the Kingdom's dislike of opposing views. Think about their success in the midst of the challenges faced by countries in the Middle East. What this initiative shows is that for any country to succeed it must plan for tomorrow, today. That is a big challenge – not to think about just today, but also about the future.

Sadly, our common habit – the poor – is that we think short term. The "what-is-in-it-for-me" type of thinking. If it doesn't benefit me then what is the point, and we reason ourselves out of it. We forget or don't realise that improving one's quality of life is a long-term process. It is a journey.

In his book *"The Millionaire Fastlane: Crack the Code to Wealth and Live Rich for a Lifetime,"* MJ DeMarco explains that a lot of the mediocre-thinking people want to be rich overnight. They see someone with all the riches and they think "I want to be like that person," which is perfectly fine. The problem with us is that we don't want to follow the process required to get to the top. We fail to appreciate that Bill Gates for instance, started with nothing but then worked his ass off to be where he is. It was a long **process** and he did not think only about himself living a fulfilling life, but he also thought about his family, his future generation.

This is what MJ DeMarco calls a PROCESS. You follow a clear roadmap to get to your destination. But most importantly, lay out the map so clearly that if you don't complete the race, someone can take over to the finish line. It is like running a relay in athletics; the starter doesn't get to the finish line but works hard from the start to set the rest of the team for success.

Our focus must be around the process, starting where we are and working our way up. There is no other way around this.

Our starting point in Africa is very low but that should not deter us because we have no choice. Imagine the situation in Sudan (which is ranked the world's poorest country, according to IMF); life in Somalia; or Zimbabweans who had to endure years of Mugabe's dictatorship (and now have to deal with the useless, granddad Mnangagwa who wants to raise the age of presidential candidates to 54 years, just imagine); how about the people of DRC? Where should they start? A South Sudanese child worries about where the next meal is going to come from; a British child on the other hand thinks about the next online game to play. That is the difference, but we still have the obligation to plan to change our fortunes for the better. And there is nothing wrong with the British child in this case because the parents planned and worked hard to achieve their goals. They earned it.

What I am trying to say is that when we plan for the "African future", we must condition our minds and understand that we (those who start the planning or the race) may not see the end results. So, my friend, set your expectations to the right starting point. This process has to start somewhere and that somewhere place is very low, and that's where we are going to have to start. Again, be mindful that it is more likely that you will not finish the race. I could die before I finish this book too, but since you are reading it I probably survived until I managed to get it published. Make sure that the roadmap is clearly mapped so that the next baton-bearer can continue where you left off. Because just like in a relay race, *if you drop that bloody baton, you will be disqualified,* and your story shall be buried with you. Remember where the riches of this world are buried, according to Les Brown? In the graves, so be mindful of that.

We must have a long-term perspective

"Success is not just the destination; it's the entire journey, every bit of it. It's not just the outcome rather it's the entire process."
~ Mohsin Ali Shaukat

Right from our birth day, our parents raise us to be responsible adults; they probably do that subconsciously, but they do. A child is raised with the long-term perspective in mind. What that means is that our parents are not raising us or should not be raising us for their benefits (that is, *a son or a daughter who is going to grow up to look after me*); they raise us to grow up and be responsible adults. I highlighted this as a weakness in Africa, where parents raise their children as some sort of an *insurance* policy for the future (the belief that the child will grow up to be the carer of the parents). That should never be the reason to justify raising your child properly.

You are probably wondering why I am telling you about raising children when I am meant to talk about planning for the future? It is because everything starts from the household level and if that foundation is not laid properly then chances are that we are condemned before we even start. They say *charity begins at home.* Frederick Douglass once said, "it is easier to build strong children than to repair broken men." That is why I am saying for Africans to make a winning start, we must start at household level.

Planning for the future is as simple as planting a tree, literally. When you drive around America or Australia or a European country, you would easily appreciate what I mean. There are huge, tall trees that were planted hundreds of years ago. There are many planted even today. Do you think the planters plant these trees for themselves to *enjoy* the oxygen and all the benefits that come with trees? That is very unlikely. I am talking about trees that are over 100 years old. The trees were planted with the future in mind. As for Africans, when we plant a tree, it is usually fruit trees that have shorter lifespans than ourselves. We want to plant a tree so that we can enjoy its fruits within a year if possible and our children will sort themselves out. And you know what they do, right? They also plant trees to benefit themselves. If you took a drive around some of the African countries, like in South Africa around the Polokwane City area in Limpopo, you will be hurt by the level of deforestation.

We do not care about the next person. When we cut trees to sell logs and firewood, we don't care about tomorrow. We just tell ourselves that someone (usually the government or charity organisations from the West) will plant the trees or we don't even think about it at all. Even if one is planted, we don't have the patience to wait for it to grow. These are the basics. We don't like waiting. We don't believe in the process. This may seem like too much focus on trees, but it is about the underlying problem we face in Africa. We just can't be bothered to worry about the future. I know this sounds too basic but that is the idea. It must be basic because it is, even though we don't get it.

The bottom line is that we don't plan too well for the future. For us to get out of the situation that we are in right now, we must start building that foundation today to ensure that our children continue that process, rather than start again. Most of African kids are forever starting from square one. When I started working I had to build my mother a house, and there is nothing wrong with that. In fact, I am very proud of myself for doing that because I have improved my mother's living standard. The problem is that a lot of us, as I mentioned earlier, would build their parents a house and then feel like they own it; they don't move out. And this is probably borne out of the fact that we have lots of siblings and my imagination is that after building houses for our parents we subconsciously feel like we cannot build a house and move out leaving our siblings to *enjoy my house*. How else can you explain that?

So, what tends to happen more often is that I would rent a house in town where I work and go "home" during the holidays. By "home" I mean my parents' place because I own that house. I built it. Over time, I get old and retire. Remember that I was living in a rented place in the city. Where do you think I would go at this stage when I don't earn a salary to pay for rent?

My wife and I did not build ourselves a house. You probably learnt at primary school that the three, bare minimum basic needs for human beings are shelter, food and clothing. But we do not plan for one of these basic needs that should be done subconsciously, literally. Guess whose responsibility it becomes now to provide his or her parents with this one basic need they don't have? My beautiful breadwinner child! Yes, they are expected and are supposed to build me, my wife and the rest of our children (and their children potentially) a house just like we did with our parents. We basically build our shelter in reverse, with no forward planning whatsoever.

The few smart ones follow this up by building their own homes, but this is just a tiny fraction. And it is a tall order. Building a house is not cheap. In other countries, it takes more than one's half their working life to pay off the mortgage. With us, it means the cycle continues from one generation to the next. After building that house for my parents I feel like I have achieved everything and forget about the future. That is where the problem lies. The *vicious cycle* continues. But who can blame me or you for being unable to build two houses? It is very hard.

Dr Mensah Otabil, a Ghanaian theologian, philanthropist, motivational speaker, entrepreneur says we must be generational thinkers. This is how he puts it:

> *"A generational thinker is one who is able to sow seeds for the future. A generational thinker is not somebody who is only committed to what he wants to enjoy today*

but somebody who says if 'I run this race, I must make sure the next generation does not run my race, the next generation must run its own race, I must empower the next generation'"

He says Africans must start thinking ahead and beyond their lifespans (the so-called, doing selfless acts) and think more than one generation ahead. It is back to planting that tree so that some time in future when we, the current generation are all dead and buried, another person with no relation to us whatsoever can sit under the shade and enjoy all the oxygen from that tree. If we don't do that, then our fate is already sealed; it will be filled with suffering and forever running our parents' races rather than ours. We are going to remain in this sad bubble of intergenerational poverty for a long time. This is painful because a lot of Africans are *travelling at a speed just close to the exit velocity* to get out of the poverty bubble. So many Africans are doing very well in their careers, but the setup and culture is holding them back and they just can't exit this poverty bubble. It is not about getting paid more. It is about getting the basics right from the start.

It goes back to the issue of parents failing to start a solid foundation for their kids. It means the children must finish or start laying the foundation that was meant to be laid by their parents (build their parents a home). After building the house for their parents, which is not an easy proposing, they have to build their own. At this stage, if they manage to build their own, they would be in their sixties and seventies. Building your first home at that age? Just think about it. Your counterparts that you completed school with in America or England – the Western world basically – would have long retired enjoying life, while the poor African dude is only starting. The problem is that after building our parents their homes, we are too exhausted to even think about our house and we just quietly move in with our old aged parents.

Long-term perspective allows us to think beyond today, and plan for our kids. That would ensure that they have a head start compared to us, their parents.

When I studied in the USA many years ago I remember the types of conversations the young American dudes would have. It was about buying shares (I had no idea what they were talking about), or things like "my savings" (the amount they had doesn't matter, but what matters is that they were talking about it), or "I moved out when I enrolled here" (moving out at your age, what a spoilt child, I would imagine, because in my mind they were not mature enough to even discuss it). These are the differences.

Break the chain

The only way out of this is to break this chain. Sometimes in life people must take drastic majors to make progress. The fact of the matter is, it is not cheap nor easy to build one house, let alone two structures; for yourself and your parents. Until we stop this madness then nothing is going to save us, and we may as well throw in the towel. What must we do then? Well, a complete and total paradigm shift is what we need.

Only build one house; yours only unless you can sincerely afford two. I mean really affording the second one, not building it on credit card.

The following question is probably going to sound too politically incorrect, but I am going to ask it still. You are entitled to your opinion. All I am doing is posing this question and you have an idea about my views on this one anyway. The question is:

> *Should we continue building big houses for our parents when we can't afford to build our own?*

My answer is a solid and bold **NO**. I say we should not. Before I get crucified and called all sorts of names, remember that ultimately the choice is yours. This is not a cast-in-concrete opinion. It is merely my opinion and that is the beauty of free speech. I can share my opinions without fear of being sent to jail, or even killed like in other countries that I am not even going to mention.

To break our generational poverty and start being generational thinkers:

> *Only build your parents a house if you have built yourself something.*

Otherwise, we are never going to make it. Dr Mensah Otabil says the problem is that Africans run double or even triple races in their lifetimes; our parents' races and our own races and potentially our grandparents' races too.

If the situation is so dire that you have to really build them something, just don't go overboard. Build something small and manageable, but not too fancy or alternatively make some minor upgrades to what they already have. What is wrong about building a one-bedroomed house with a small kitchen, sitting room and a bathroom?

When I started working I built my mother a full-sized three-bedroom house. She didn't need a 3-bedroomed house, but I still built it because I was thinking about my siblings too. Then I had to keep staying with my mother and my siblings even after I got married. That, my friend, is not healthy for a relationship. Just take my word for it.

As I said, I could have easily built my mother a nice unit. I could not because we tend to worry too much about what others would say about us if we don't build our parents *proper* houses. Building a house is not the only way you can help your parents. I will expand on this shortly.

In the Western world for instances (and I am sorry to keep referring to the West but who else can we compare ourselves against if we want to move ahead?), a mortgage payment takes 20 to 30 years to pay off. If you start working, say when you are 24 years old then you would probably buy your house after 4 years, that is, when you are 28 years old (you need a bit of time to save for your down payment or deposit). That means by the time you finish paying for the mortgage you would be around 55 years old on average. If they were doing it the African style, that would be the age they finish paying for their parents' house. At that stage, do you think anyone would think about getting another mortgage? I didn't think so either. But for them, that is not an issue they have to worry about, thank God. If this was the case, then there would be too many poor people in the West. They are fortunate that they don't have to run their parents' races along with theirs. It is hard dealing with your challenges let alone your parents'.

You probably are wondering, what do we do with our parents then? Very good question and there is no simple answer to this challenge. As far as I am concerned, there are a few options that one can consider and again they are not perfect solutions. Be mindful that we are trying to salvage a potentially bleak situation here, so there wouldn't be a perfect solution. Compromises must be made especially on the parents' side if they want to see their grandchildren prosper. A lot of people must sacrifice a bit and that's how successful people get to the top. A lot of sacrifices are made, leaving many people angry and upset along the way.

Below are some of the options that I believe we must pursue.

The first option is:

Let your parents continue living at their current address – this is probably the best and easiest option to consider. If it is at their parents', then so be it. The key is that they are looked after and have a roof over their heads. It may not be a fancy dwelling but believe me, the alternative for you is worse. I know some of you are thinking, *"what a cold, sick, remorseless, heartless person this guy is!"* But I promise you that this is probably the best option available to us if we really want to get out of this entrapment. Please don't read this and think I am encouraging people not to look after their parents. Nothing can be further from the truth. If you should build something, anything at all, make it very small and manageable. The point is that you don't want to be in a life-long debt that you end up living behind for your children to continue paying when you are dead. Don't you think that is even more cruel? A lot of people would choose to ignore this reality.

Consider the following true story:

> *A few years ago, when I was working for a mining company in Botswana, a lot of people lost their jobs following an industrial action – a fancy way of a strike basically. That company that I worked for had and I believe still has one of the best and cheapest (subsidised) accommodation in the whole country if not Africa. We paid about $60 per month for a 4-bedroomed house, with*

double garage, fitted kitchen, guest house (we called it a servants' quarters because that was where our babysitters stayed).

The houses were huge and that gave a lot of us a false sense of security, where we believed that we owned homes. With that security, a lot of us, would build houses for our parents at the village as is the norm. Some didn't build anything because they couldn't afford to build for their parents, but the worst part of it was that they did not build their own either. Anyway, once that house was out of the way – the one for the parents if you happened to build one – you feel like you have achieved it all in life. On school holidays, we would go home for a few days and stay with the parents. There didn't seem to be anything wrong with that arrangement. We were all conforming to the culture.

Then, the mother of all strikes took the country by storm and the miners were not spared. A lot of people lost their jobs and were given a few days to vacate the company houses; 10 days at most. Ten days is a fairly long time to organise transport (a moving company) to transfer your belongings to your house. The trouble was, most of the fired employees had nowhere to go. They either didn't build their own houses or if they built for their parents, the houses were not big enough to accommodate them along with their fancy furniture from the town. So, there was this embarrassing situation where we had so many former employees with fancy cars, nice furniture but no homes.

When the grace period expired, the company hired trucks to literally haul people and their belongings out of their (mine's) properties. It was sad and embarrassing.

What I am trying to highlight here is simple and that is, if we raise our kids well and accept that when they finish school and start working, their first order of business is to build their own houses, then we would be setting Africa on a path to maturity and success. A path to prosperity.

That is why I say, do not rush to building your parents a house before you look at your situation. If you can afford two houses, which is seldom the case, then who am I to tell you how to spend your money? I am just saying be mindful of this issue.

The best thing you can do for your children is to ensure that they don't do your dirty work. Set them up for success. That is the first step towards prosperity for Africa. It starts from household level, where we reduce too much reliance on government, allowing the government to use the resources on better programs and initiatives rather than welfare.

That is my case against building houses for your parents before you build one for yourself. And again, do it only if you can afford it, not based on "what would people say?" The key thing is to have that discussion with your parents and make them understand. Believe me, all of them understand and they will support you for that. They love you and their grandchildren more. This would also reduce your burden and give you the ability to provide for your parents.

You can always visit www.makeafricabetter.info and have your say. All I am doing here is start a conversation and some of you may have better proposals.

The second option is:

Build them a small house – I am talking a portable one with one bedroom, a kitchen, bathroom and a sitting room. Remember the idea is to make sure that you don't burden yourself at the expense of your family (spouse and kids).

The last option to consider is:

Old aged care facilities or simply a rental property – I know we are not there yet when it comes to proper facilities for old aged care, but this is an option that needs to be considered moving forward. Remember that it does not have to be fancy. In fact, if you are looking for a business idea, this is one that can be exploited. If you can have your aged parents stay at a facility where they can be well taken care of, then that must be an option worth considering.

It would be much cheaper than building them a new house and feeding them at the same time. You may even be able to better support them with other critical basic needs that you wouldn't otherwise afford if you were to build them a house. Things like private medical cover, life insurance, clean water, and so forth. These are the things we are not able to provide to our parents because we are so deep in debt that we can't afford providing for these important lifesaving programs. This (lack of medical insurance) leads to our low life expectancies in Africa. The countries with the lowest life expectancies are in Africa, with Chad at 50.6 years. Just imagine, people dying at 50? I am not saying this idea of aged care facilities are going to increase this, but what I am saying is that it would give people "extra" cash that can be spent on healthcare.

Anyway, the reason I say this idea is for the future is that Africans still don't embrace old aged care facilities. These facilities are frowned upon; people look at these with the attitude that says you are *washing your hands and throwing your parents away.* More like you don't want the responsibility of looking after your parents and want nothing to do with them. That is a completely corrupted and poor mindset. In fact, some facilities provide much better care than the children would offer because they have the resources (trained personnel and facilities) to care for the aged.

For me, my friends, these are the options that we must pursue, otherwise we are going to continue running this never-ending race. For me this is the *exit velocity* required for us to escape this bubble or a vicious poverty cycle that we are stuck in.

In closing, do the following:

- Whatever you do, think long term my fellow African friends. Do not do something just for your personal gain, but for the future generation whether related to you or not. Like planting a tree. It benefits more than your close relatives;

- Break the cycle. Talk to your parents and bring it to their attention that even though you may be working and earning a decent salary they must understand that your family (spouse and kids) are your top priority. I can assure you that your parents' love is unconditional and they will support you for that. Understand this point right please; I am not saying don't look after your parents. All I am saying is that look after them and help as much as you can but don't do that to impress others. Try to make sure that you break the cycle. Make it your life mission that your children should never have to care for you. If you realise that you don't have enough money to maintain the same lifestyle, cut back please. Don't make your children fill the gap.

Chapter 8 Summary

- Each one of us must run their own race – I personally think this is another one of those big issues that is holding Africans back. It is never easy to deal with our own challenges, let alone our parents'. Our culture makes it hard to focus on just our own life challenges. I am not implying that we must forget our culture and adopt the West's, but we have to move on with the times. The idea that I can build my parents a huge house that is the envy of neighbours and also be able to build a decent one for my own family is just a dream. Yes, some can afford that, and I mean a small fraction of Africans;

- For Africa to prosper, the current generation must set the future generation for success. This is an obligation that we must fulfil. I am not talking about building a new rocket to land the first African on the moon or anything like that. I am talking about raising our kids with the knowledge that when they complete their studies they must move on with their lives and not be burdened by us. If I fail to plan for my retirement, then that shouldn't be my children's problem. They can help if they want. They don't have to.

CHAPTER 9 – We must focus on the basics

"We are not helpless. We all have the ability to make this world a better place. We can start with small steps, one day at a time." ~ Wayne Gerard Trotman

"Big things have small beginnings." ~ Promethus

Below is a typical conversation between two grownups wearing suits and ties, well educated in a city like Pretoria in South Africa.

> **You**: Hey EC, come on mate, why are you throwing that coke can on the ground just like that my bro? Don't you realise that you hutting our economy, let alone the environment?
>
> **Me**: Hey "your name," I am creating employment for the guys who pick trash. If I don't litter they will be out of work. See, I am smart (pointing my finger to head to signal that I am thinking). And what is the environment? I just threw this on the ground. I am not hurting anyone;
>
> **You**: It doesn't look right at all;
>
> **Me**: What do you mean it doesn't look right? There is trash everywhere you look. It's not like I am the only one doing it. We all do it.

This is not a joke. In fact, there doesn't have be litter lying around before someone throws a can on the ground. It happens too often in Gaborone, the capital city of Botswana at a shopping centres. Someone walking on a clean open paved area, finishing his drink and just casually throwing a can. So, yes we still have people who think like this in 2019; very short-sighted and self-centred individuals who couldn't care less about the next person. The type that would see a big thorn or a sharp nail on the road and not be bothered to warn other road users about the hazard. And frankly, there are too many of us who fall in this category.

Don't you think it is crazy that we still have people employed by the government or the local town council, whose job is nothing other than litter picking? I am talking about a civil servant, as they are referred, going to work in the morning, grabbing a trash bag and a trash picker, and taking a walk along streets and shopping malls to pick rubbish. I am talking about litter where people throw cans, paper, plastic, and all the nasty dirty crap you can imagine (some of it can't be mentioned in this book). You would see men and women wearing uniform holding *trash pokers* (I call it a poker because it is a piece of hardened thick wire with a pointed end like a spear) and black plastic bags walking streets picking litter. All they do is poke an empty drink can that was thrown on the ground by an adult and putting it in a trash bag. I am not demeaning these people. They are doing wonderful jobs under difficult conditions. But I believe this is a complete waste of human resources.

If you are from outside the continent of Africa and took a walk on a busy street in an African town (or at least most African towns) you will be shocked at the amount of trash littering the streets; anything from cans, plastic, paper, scrap electronics, glass, tyres, bats, soccer balls; I mean everything. I am telling you, if you name it, I guarantee you that it would be found for you on the street.

In some instances, if you are not careful you would get the shock of your life with used water landing on your head and wetting your entire body from someone throwing it over the fence. Yeah, just like that. Walking and minding your own business, you would be awoken or scared by a splash of dirty water landing on you, in front or behind you.

Things like throwing rubbish out the window of a moving car doesn't seem to bother anyone. Chances are that as you throw that can out the window it will find its companion on the street where it lands. Louis CK, an American comedian, once joked that when he walks around New York he just throws 'sh*t' on the sidewalk because New York is a trash dump.

The point I am trying to make here is that due to the amount of rubbish around us in most African cities and towns, it usually doesn't feel like such a bad idea to throw an empty drink can on the ground when you are done with it. If in an unlikely event you dared to ask someone to pick up their rubbish, I don't think you would enjoy the vitriol sent back to you. You would be told to be respectful or asked who you think you are.

Street pissers

Emptying a male gallbladder on a street in a heavily populated area is so common in Africa to a point that it is not even noticed. The only people who notice are tourists from the so-called first world countries. There is no shame about a grown-up man in a suit, carrying a laptop bag and a business briefcase stopping by the side of the road to take a piss, and while at it, answer a phone call. Then a few metres later, shake an unsuspecting friend's hand with the same unwashed hand that was busy handling some serious business earlier. It doesn't matter anyway because the recipient's hand was probably active performing a similar act a few minutes earlier. So, it is like for like and why should we be ashamed of performing a natural act in the open, whether people are watching or not? Nature's call must be respected and acted upon. These are legitimate arguments for us to do our business in the open. How unfortunate! Sometimes women walking from behind or in the opposite direction are forced to stop, wait and look away to show "some respect" to the dirty guy urinating on the street.

This must stop. But Madiba EC my friend, whether I take a piss in the open or not, my life isn't going to change. I mean, *"it is only a peer buddy and it will dry,"* or *"I need something to improve my life and pissing or not pissing on the street is the least of my worries right now."*

The act of not urinating on the street is not going to make you rich or anything like that. It is not going to address your concerns about where your next meal is going to come from. It is the same as the act of throwing or not throwing that empty can of beer out into the open instead of binning it. The important thing is not the act itself but the habit. The type of a person you are becoming by stopping those bad habits. The way you think. Your appreciation of the small things. If all of us do these small things right, the sum of these seemingly little acts are gigantic gains. It is important to understand that it is these *small* habits that go a long way in defining us as either civil or uncivil.

Start with just one 'can' at a time

There is a proverb by Lao Tzu, an ancient Chinese philosopher and writer that says, *a journey of a thousand miles begins with a single step.* And I also say, start with that one piece of trash, whether it is a can or plastic bag or even a gum. Anything. Consider the following hypothesis;

- We all stop throwing rubbish everywhere for a period of six months or even up to one year. Just religiously binning all the rubbish without fail;

- The hardworking guys who pick litter continue picking whatever is already on the ground for that same duration. Again, religiously picking litter and sweeping entire streets without slowing down.

What do you think the net effect of this would be? Obviously, I am just putting a theory out there and assuming that the people who pick up the trash continue working as hard as they would normally do. If these conditions are met, I bet there would be very little to nothing left for the town council to pick on the street. There would be some "fresh air" and a sense of relief and belief within ourselves. It is like being at work with your office table well organised. It has that feeling of professionalism and fresh look. You can try it. If you have a disorganised office desk with papers and files all over, just clear everything off the table and organise it nicely; you will feel fresh.

I never used to make my bed. When I went to sleep I would take off my pants where I stood and put on my pyjamas, get under the sheets and sleep. In the morning I would just pick up the pants where I left them when I put on the pyjamas and leave the bed in mess. When evening time arrived, it was the same routine. When I started making the bed, I felt good. It feels like there is fresh air in the room. That's what small acts like that do to you.

Back to the scenario above with regards to cleaning our streets, the short-term pain would be that some civil servants would lose their jobs, assuming all the rubbish is picked up. The bigger picture is that the government would have extra money to spend on better initiatives like improving school facilities, for instance or whatever it may be. That is not what I am trying to address here, i.e., how the government should spend the money. All I want is to focus on what we have control over. What we both know is that money spent to pay people to pick up rubbish is just money wasted. It has the unintended consequences of making people complacent and continue with the bad behaviour of not binning their rubbish because someone is going to pick that. There are no benefits or if there are any, they are temporary because that litter picked today would be replaced by another the following day. We must start looking at money spent as an investment. Spending it on picking litter every day of the year is not good investment.

This sounds very simplistic and rightfully so, because it is simple. All it takes is doing the basics, hence *'a journey of a thousand miles begins with a single step'*. Why think about fixing a car if you can't fix a bicycle? Start small and build your way up.

A South African businessman called <u>Vusi Thembekwayo</u> says we must "be patient to start small while thinking big." See a response to a question he was asked by a young South African who said he was rejected by major corporations and banks when he tried to borrow money to start an egg farming business. He said:

> *"We were actually confronted with a few of these cases. Often people come up with an end idea and want to get there without following a process. I often use the alphabet as an example. To get from A-Z, you need to go through each alphabet. And so, it is with entrepreneurship.*
>
> *"Young black entrepreneurs often want to skip the process and I tell them that they need to start with what*

they've got. Get the small things working and slowly build a track record.

"No one is going to give you money to get you where you are to where you want to be. You have to build small successes and build a track record. What do you know about eggs? Get into egg retail perhaps: build commercial skills, learn about margins, and learn who the end user is. Generate cash. Create discipline. After you have been selling eggs for a certain time, go to a funder and show your proof of credibility and gravitas.

"Take my graded entrepreneur process, instead of looking for blue sky funding. Find the right funding at the right level. Start small with 1 000 eggs and then get working capital funding to produce 10 000 eggs.

"So many people want to start at A and then get to Z without any process. They think Virgin happened in a day. Richard Branson started one business, then a few more. He had some failures and closed some businesses down. Then he started building again and eventually became successful. That's how it works." (source, <u>YouTube</u>).

I know the preceding notes were about entrepreneurship, but the concept is the same. Start small by doing the basics first. And for Africans, that means starting with a piece of litter or picking a can of coke thrown on the ground. Start with clearing the streets one can at a time. Start picking a piece of paper. Stop throwing empty cans out in the open but bin them. Stop peering on the street. I cannot imagine anything easier. The good thing about doing the basics and making them a habit is that you eventually do them without thinking. It becomes second nature, more like breathing. When that happens, it means you start thinking about something a level higher; something more important. Imagine looking at the ground and seeing clean sand not covered by trash. As you look at the barren ground you start realising that something is missing on that fertile soil. Maybe some lawn or trees. You get motivated to plant a tree. When that tree grows, you realise that you are onto something great and more trees get planted. You start thinking in a positive manner. That's all it takes.

What we must focus on are the small habits. Have some responsibility. Have some accountability in our actions. Then naturally we will start worrying about marginally bigger things. That is the process. We should start with these smaller habits and there would be natural progression. When the streets are clean and it becomes our way of life, that's it. It is done.

I am appealing to you all my beautiful African brothers and sisters, the sons and daughters of the soil, let us start this journey.

Chapter 9 Summary

- Start small because those small acts add up very quickly;

- Do the basics and everything else will fall in place.

Conclusions

Remember that you reap what you sow, and the great Jim Rohn went even further to say you always reap more than what you saw. If you plant one seed of sorghum you get hundreds of seeds. The seeds I am referring to are what I outlined in the preceding chapters. I am going to summarise all that in the next few paragraphs.

Education

In my opinion, everything outlined in this book revolves around the topic about education. Education is a rich word that covers a wide range of subjects. Do you think I would stop littering the streets if I don't understand the impact that that act has on the environment or our economy? I doubt it. That is why I believe it is very important for our future generation to get the right kind of education. The type that make them understand that there is more to knowledge than knowing that one plus one equals two. It is upon us, their parents to contribute to this effort because the formal education we have today does not prepare our children well for the future.

Productivity

When someone talks about cheap labour in Africa, the tendency is for people to think in terms of an hourly rate, which is wrong. As in January 2019 Beijing's minimum wage was $2.77 per hour, compared to around $0.68 per hour Botswana. For a company to set shop in any country, there are many factors that the leadership of that company consider and one of those is cheap labour because it helps their bottom-line. Politics, corruption and many other factors are considered of course.

Botswana is considered one of the least corrupt countries in the world; not Africa but the world. It is politically stable, and the level of crime is one of the lowest in Africa. The question is, why would Ford America set plant in China instead of Botswana where the labour cost is 4 times lower than in China? Like I said, many other factors are considered, but let's assume that all other factors are the same. It is down to productivity. For the same hourly rate, a Chinese is more productive. That is where we are losing the battle. The cost of labour in Botswana and many African nations is significantly higher than in China mainly due to our low productivity. For us to attract any foreign investment, we must pull up our socks. Again, education plays an important role here. If our children and student can't grasp this simple logic, then we wouldn't make any progress.

We don't have to forget, but we must forgive

If you are one of those people who always remind others about their mistakes, chances are that you are not successful in life. You are the "grudge-holder." How long are we going to live in the past and continue blaming our white friends about their bad deeds? We don't have to forget, but we must forgive. There are no "buts" about this one. That is one of the cheapest decisions we can make. Our anger and painting all white people as racist when they try to show us our failings is not going to help us.

Conformance

If it isn't broke, don't fix it. Similarly, the converse is true. That is, if it is broke, fix it. We know that our approach to life is faulty (poverty, crime, corruption, poor sanitation – you name it) and yet for God-knows-why, we continue on the same path that our parents, grandparents and others before them followed. Just think about it for a moment; don't you think that's insane?

Life Choices

Deciding to conform to the norm is a life choice.

If you peer on the street or litter the surrounding, that is a life choice.

Life choice is blaming everyone else but yourself for your failings.

Most of the topics outlined in this book point to these two words – Life Choices.

All I am saying here is that *make the right choices.*

Entitlement and Breadwinners

If we could all live our lives with the knowledge that this world doesn't owe us a thing, our planet would be a better place. I have an unfavourable opinion about people who believe that they can live as parasites where the government must do everything for them or that there is a breadwinner in the family and they don't have to worry about their next meal. Each one of us must be independent. I know that some people can't manage because of health issues or any unfortunate circumstance beyond their control and these people deserve our support. But if you are capable of standing on your feet to do something worthwhile for yourself, then you don't deserve our sympathy if you stay home and go hungry. Just don't be too picky of what jobs you can do. You don't have that luxury if you are unemployed.

Think beyond today

My wish is for my children to live shackle-free from my past life choices. I don't want them to run my race because it is hard enough to run your own race. I hope this makes sense? If you didn't know what a rat race is, then look around you (that is if you are in Africa). The situation we find ourselves in is a good example of a rat race. The endless problems that seem to be getting worse with each passing generation. There is only one way to get out of this situation and that is think beyond today. Think about the next person after you. If you are not happy about your current situation, the least you can do is share your experiences with your children so that they don't repeat the same mistakes.

We must value ourselves ...

... because if we don't, nobody is going to. I spoke about skin whitening creams that a lot of Africans are using to look lighter or whiter. The belief being that doing so would make one look beautiful. It is okay to want to "look beautiful" and that is not the issue here. The problem is the value you place on your appearance as opposed to your being. If you are an idiot, whitening your skin is not going to change that. In fact, it probably removes all doubt that people had about your intelligence or your IQ level. You can only find peace if you value yourself.

Do the basics

The good thing about doing the basics is that it is usually cheap. Before you start a large-scale farming business, don't you think it is best to learn the basics first? There are no shortcuts to doing things right. Start with a garden in your backyard, learn the challenges and slowly start selling excess to your neighbours. That is how you start. If you have running water and a 20mx20m area in the backyard, there is no reason you should be buying watermelon or spinach. It is that simple, believe me.

Bonus Chapter

I thought I should throw is some business ideas that you may try wherever you are in Africa. Again, learn how it is done first before spending your hard-earned cash.

- Tutoring (Online or face-to-face) – when I was younger still attending school, I was very good with maths and science subjects (other than biology, or so I believed – the power of subconscious mind). I am sure there are many kids who would have spent a few bucks to tap into my knowledge. You too can if you are good in any particular subject.

- Music Lessons – maybe you are good with a guitar or some music instrument. How about you offer that service to people who may be interested. I know you would get some cash because I spent some money a few years ago trying to learn a guitar. I just didn't take if far, which I regret, because *I didn't have the time.* But it is something that I am still planning to pursue.

- Gardening – don't follow the crowd and start charging excessive prices to help people maintain their homes. If you have good gardening and landscaping skills, why not use them at price?

- Courier or Delivery Services – packages delivery service is crap in most parts of Africa and I bet there are people who would be willing to pay some money when they know that their packages would be delivered on time. Like in Botswana, to order an item from China to Gaborone, it takes 3 days for the package to arrive in Gaborone. For the package to be delivered from a warehouse in Gaborone to a residential place can take a week. This is not an exaggeration.

- Proofreading and editing – you probably are good with English (I say English because that is the commonly spoken language). You can help people with their blogs or books and make some cash.

- Exercise instructor – obesity and overweight are some of the challenges that are affecting a lot of people in Africa. If you are good with some exercises that can help people lose some of those pounds, this can be a lucrative business. This can be done as a meetup sort of a thing where people meet at a football ground or something like that and you lead them in exercise. This is easily done as a subscription service.

- Buying and reselling on eBay – this is basically online retailing and it doesn't have to be eBay. It's just that eBay is common and if you are starting this could be a good starting point. There are a lot of people in the developed world that are willing to buy handmade items from Africa. This is a business opportunity that can be exploited. Better still, if you have a skill of your own as in crafting then you can make a fortune by selling your products.

- Creating custom clothing – this can tie up to the online selling mentioned above.

- Website Developer – the world is now connected via the Internet and if you are good with creativity and web designs then this can be a lucrative business.

- Farming – I reserved this one for last. If you were to do this one properly, following the right processes, believe me when I tell you that this would be like mining gold. Botswana imports more than 70% of its food requirement. Yes, farming is tough and all that. Everything is. If you were to follow the process by learning how it is done, then there is no reason why you can't make it.

Recommended Reading

The Richest man in Babylon - George S. Clason

Think and Grow Rich – Napoleon Hill

The Magic of Thinking Big – Dr David J. Schwartz

The Millionaire Fastlane: Crack the Code to Wealth and Live Rich for a Lifetime – MJ DeMarco

The Miracle Morning the 6 Habits That Will Transform Your Life Before 8AM – Hal Elrod

Eat that Frog! – Brian Tracy

The Future ...

This book focused more on outlining some of the main challenges we face in Africa and what we can do to address them. The next book I am working on is going to focus a lot more on behaviour and the subconscious mind.

I am learning a lot about this topic (subconscious mind) and I believe with my knowledge of my continent, I would be able to dissect this issue, link it well with our challenges and come up with ideas on how we can use the power of our subconscious mind to change our beliefs system for a better future.

Thank you for your time and I hope it was worthwhile.

About Madiba EC

I, Madiba EC was born in a rural, poor African village called Tsetsebjwe in eastern Botswana. I am the oldest in the family and have 4 siblings, lost 2 siblings (my older brother and my immediate little sister). I am married to Beauty Madiba and we have three beautiful children.

All I can tell you is that I have matured into a man that I am proud of. I may have disappointed a few people along the way but if I did, it wasn't intentional. I am sorry. Are we cool? No grudges, right?

I try to think positive, even though I occasionally have those negative thoughts finding their way into my life, I always try to push them out.

Printed in Great Britain
by Amazon